OSIP MANDELSHTAM
The Eyesight of Wasps

The translator:

James Greene was born in Berlin in 1938. He took a degree in French and Russian at Oxford, and studied Psychology and English Literature at London University. His poems and translations have appeared in a number of journals in the UK and United States.

In 1985 he won first prize in the British Comparative Literature Association's translation competition for his versions of Fernando Pessoa, and in 1986 second prize in the TLS/Cheltenham Festival of Literature poetry competition. Earlier versions of some of the poems included in the present volume were published by Elek (1977) and Granada (1980), and read at the National Theatre, the Mermaid, Riverside Studios, at both the Oxford and Cambridge Poetry Festivals, and on Radio 3. Three of his translations of Mandelshtam are included in *The Oxford Book of Verse in English Translation*.

OSIP MANDELSHTAM

The Eyesight of Wasps

Poems translated by
JAMES GREENE

Forewords by Nadezhda Mandelshtam and Donald Davie
Introduction by Donald Rayfield

with Russian texts in appendix

A Sandstone Book
Ohio State University Press
Columbus

For R. F. H. and A. W.
who kept me at it

Translations, Translator's Preface and Notes
Copyright © James Greene 1989

'Osip Mandelshtam: An Introduction' by Donald Rayfield
Copyright © Angel Books 1989

Russian texts of Osip Mandelshtam's poems
Copyright by Inter-Language Literary Associates, 1967

Published in the U.S.A. by
The Ohio State University Press

Published in Great Britain by Angel Books

Library of Congress Cataloging-in-Publication Data

Mandel'shtam, Osip, 1891-1938.
  The eyesight of wasps.

  "A Sandstone book."
  Bibliography: p.
  I. Greene, James, 1938-   II. Title.
PG3476.M355A24   1988   891.71'3   88-17806
ISBN 0-8142-0478-3

Printed and bound in Great Britain

*The paper in this book is acid-free and meets the
guidelines for permanence and durability of
the Committee on Production Guidelines for Book Longevity of the
Council on Library Resources.*

Fine fingers quiver;
A fragile body breathes:
A boat sliding across
Fathomless silent seas.

1909

Few live for Always.
But if the passing moment makes you anxious
Your lot is terror and your house precarious!

1912

And alone I read,
Infinity, your primer:
Your wild leafless herbal,
Logarithm-table of prodigious roots.

1933

Your eyebrows, like poppies, open up a dangerous path.
Why am I in love like a janissary
With this tiny volatile red,
The pitiful crescent of your lips?

1934

Angelic criminal, insolent schoolboy,
In the midst of the Gothic a villain:
He spat on the law like a spider –
Incomparable François Villon.

1937

Aortas fill with blood.
A murmur rings through the ranks:
– I was born in '94,
I was born in '92 . . .
And, clutching the worn-out year of my birth,
Herded wholesale with the herd,
I whisper through anaemic lips:
I was born in the night of January the second and third
In the unreliable year
Of eighteen-ninety something or other,
And the centuries surround me with fire.

1937

Contents

From TRISTIA (1922)

From POEMS (1928)

Two poems published in NOVYY MIR, 1931 and 1932

Poems published posthumously

Foreword by
Nadezhda Mandelshtam

I think that the most difficult task in the world is the translation of verses, particularly of a true poet, in whose verses there is no discrepancy between the form and the content (or meaning) – both of them always new and but a bit different (with no great disparity between them) – and where the ego of the poet is always strikingly felt. Marina Tsvetayeva said she could write as Mandelshtam did but that she didn't want to. She was a great poet but she was greatly mistaken. She could be influenced by Mayakovsky and Pasternak and remain Tsvetayeva because they were *innovators* and therefore easily aped. But Mandelshtam composed verses *in tradition*, which is far more difficult to imitate.

Mr Robert Lowell's translations are very free; Mr Paul Celan's into German also free. But both are a very far cry from the original text. As far as I know the translations of Mr Greene are the best I ever saw. I can't give my opinion about the Italian translations, as I don't know Italian as well as English, French and German. As for Elsa Triolet's, they are as naive and vulgar as she was.

Mandelshtam said that the contents are squeezed from the form as water from a sponge.* If the sponge is dry, there would be no moisture at all. So, to render the content – which Mr Greene has succeeded in doing – is to give, in a way, the form or harmony, the harmony which *can't* be rendered in translation, the harmony which is quite simple and at the same time mysteriously complicated. Poetry is a mystery.

Nadezhda Mandelshtam, 1976

---

* See Translator's Preface, page 16, for discussion of Mandelshtam's statement in its original context.

Foreword by
Donald Davie

Of Mandelshtam's *Octets*, Robert Chandler has said that 'the informing energy of the poem stems from, is a part of, the universal impulse to form, which leads equally to the creation of a petal or a cupola, the pattern of a group of sailing-boats or a poem.' And Mr Chandler may be right. Yet as I worked at the *Octets**** it seemed to me on the contrary that Mandelshtam was distinguishing one kind of form from another, and was celebrating only those forms that are 'bent in', arced, the form of a foetus or a cradle, specifically *not* the open-ended and discontinuous mere 'pattern' (rather than 'form') that a group of sailing-boats may fall into.

I stress this because I am inclined to see in it the clue to what is distinctive about this poet, and what is distinctively daunting about the challenge he presents to his translators. If I am right, Mandelshtam's poems themselves yearn towards, and achieve, forms that are 'bent in', rounded, sounding a full bell-note. Moreover, because what the poems say is at one with the forms they find for the saying, we see why it is that, as Clarence Brown tells us, for Mandelshtam 'cognition' is always 'recognition' – *re*-cognition, a return upon itself, a 'coming round again'.

And nothing else, so far as I can see, will enable us to reconcile Anna Akhmatova's firm declaration, 'he had no poetic forerunners', with his widow's no less firm admonition: 'Mandelshtam . . . unlike *innovators* such as Mayakovsky and Pasternak . . . composed verses *in tradition*, which is far more difficult to imitate'. What sort of a poet can this be, who is 'traditional' and yet has 'no poetic forerunners'? We solve this riddle by saying that in his techniques Mandelshtam was indeed unprecedented, yet the techniques were made to serve a *form* – why not say simply, a *beauty*? – that rejoiced in calling upon every precedent one might think of, from Homer to Ovid, to the builders of Santa Sophia, to Dante and Ariosto and Racine. For it is true, surely: the sort of form to which Mandelshtam vows himself alike in nature and in art, the form of the bent-in and the

---

* Donald Davie's version of Mandelshtam's long poem *The Octets* was published in *Agenda*, Vol. 14 No. 2, 1976.

rounded-upon-itself, is the most ancient and constant of all European understandings of the beautiful – it is what long ago recognised in the circle the image of perfection. This profoundly traditional strain and aspiration in Mandelshtam explains why the Russia of his lifetime is seldom imaged directly in his poetry, and why, when it is so imaged, the image is overshadowed by others from ancient Greece or from Italy; it explains why domes and cupolas and shells (whether whorled or scalloped) appear in his poetry so often; and it explains why the hackneyed figures of the sky as a dome and a vault, and of the sea as curved round the earth's curve, appear in that poetry so insistently and with such otherwise unexplained potency. If we were to call Mandelshtam 'classical' this is what we might mean, or what we ought to mean. And nothing is further from what may reasonably be seen as the characteristic endeavour of the Western European and American of this century, in all the arts – that is to say, the finding of beauty in the discontinuous and the asymmetrical, the open-ended and indeed the adventitious.

Just here arises the peculiarly extreme difficulty of translating Mandelshtam into English. Before James Greene's, the most readable and accomplished translation we had was by W. S. Merwin, done in collaboration with Clarence Brown. But this was, necessarily and properly, an *American* translation; a translation, that's to say, into that one of the twentieth-century idioms which is, and has been ever since Walt Whitman, and even in such an untypical American as Pound, pre-eminently vowed to the open-ended and the discontinuous. Yet Mandelshtam is the most 'European' of all Russian poets since Pushkin. How could Merwin have succeeded? Yet he did – to the extent that he does indeed bring over, for a public that has not and cannot have any immediate access to the Mediterranean fountains of European consciousness, as much of Mandelshtam as can survive that oceanic passage. Here however was a chance for that one of the English-speaking idioms which *is* part of the European consciousness: could the British idiom achieve what by its very nature the American could not? James Greene had his own difficulties; for current British idioms, in so far as they respect the integrity of the verse-line and the verse-stanza (and plainly that was what was involved), characteristically give *pattern* instead of *form*, or else – to put it another way – they preserve the arc of the poem's form only by 'filling in', by not having the content of the poem pressing up against the curve of its form with equal pressure at every point. (The opposite danger, which I have not escaped in my versions, is of packing the content against the verse-line so tightly that the verse is felt to be straining and, as it were, bursting at the seams.) James Greene was equal to the challenge. His measuring up to it is shown in the first place by his daring to do what every verse-translator must have guiltily felt he ought to do, but was afraid of doing – that's to say, by leaving untranslated those parts of poems for which he could find no equivalent in English verse that carried authority. His more positive virtues – particularly in finding English near-equivalents for the punning resemblances in sound which, for Mandelshtam as for Pasternak, function as structural principles, given the richly orchestrated nature of Russian – can be appreciated only by those who can check back against the Russian originals.

Here for the first time we have a faithful version, not of Mandelshtam, but of as much of Mandelshtam as this scrupulous translator is prepared to stand by – faithful as never before, because as never before there is no line of the Russian poems that is not made *poetry* in English. Previous British versions have been wooden; this one *rings* – it is bronze, properly Roman bronze.

Donald Davie, 1977
Stanford University, California

14

Translator's Preface

[Mandelshtam] had no poetic forerunners – wouldn't that be something worth thinking about for his biography? In all of world poetry I know of no other such case. We know the sources of Pushkin and Blok, but who will tell us where that new, divine harmony, Mandelshtam's poetry, came from?

Anna Akhmatova

Translation it is that openeth the window, to let in the light; that breaketh the shell, that we may eat the kernel.

King James Bible, 1611:
'The Translators to the Reader'

The question of how to translate – should translations, like wives and husbands, be 'faithful' or 'free'? – has continued to be controversial ever since the literal-minded Gavin Douglas rebuked Caxton for his 'counterfeit' of Virgil, and Dryden (two hundred years later) aligned himself cautiously on the other side: '. . . something must be lost in all Transfusion, that is, in all Translation.' Where I add *'from'* to the number in brackets at the bottom of each poem, this is to indicate that, in these versions, lines (and sometimes whole stanzas) have been omitted, in an attempt to produce poems that work *in English*, as Pound's transformations of Rihaku do. Occasionally I compress two of Mandelshtam's poems into one. (Boris Bukhstab wrote in 1929: '. . . in Mandelshtam's poetry every stanza is practically autonomous . . . Any stanza can be discarded or added.'* This was not intended by him as a criticism. I leave it to the reader to work out how or if this can be reconciled with Clarence Brown's statement concerning No. 39 that a poem for Mandelshtam 'is a structure of words that support and oppose each other, as a cathedral is a structure of stones that support each other.')

Mandelshtam's poems are rhymed and strictly metrical, *Whoever finds a horseshoe* being the only exception. I have often had to eschew

---

* *Russian Literature Triquarterly*, No. 1, 1971.

rhyme (but not half-rhyme, internal rhymes or assonance), and have tried to feel my way towards what might be the right rhythm for English.

To the non-Russian-speaking reader who wants to know about the relation between Mandelshtam's metres (which I have not consciously set out to re-enact), length of line, etc., and mine, I can only say: 'decisions' of this kind are made intuitively; *total* 'faithfulness', were it possible – the 'same' metre, rhyme-scheme, pattern of sounds, number of syllables, line-length, etc., etc. – would be an absurdity. Translations that attempt 'faithfulness' to metre and rhyme-scheme of the originals are usually *un*faithful in a more important sense – they fail to have the same effect on an English reader as the original on a reader in the original language.

In her Foreword Nadezhda Mandelshtam writes: 'Mandelshtam said that the contents are squeezed from the form as water from a sponge.' She is wrong. Here is a translation of what Mandelshtam in fact wrote in his essay *Conversation about Dante*:

> There is not just one form in Dante, but a multitude of forms. One is squeezed out of another . . . He himself says:
> *Io premerei di mio concetto il suco* (Inferno, XXXII, 4) –
> 'I would squeeze the juice out of my idea, out of my conception.' That is, he considers form something that is squeezed out, not as that which serves as a covering.
> In this way, strange as it may seem, form is squeezed out of the content-conception which, as it were, envelops the form . . .
> But only if a sponge or rag is wet can something be wrung from it . . . We will never squeeze any form out of it (the conception) unless the conception is already a form itself.

R. F. Holmes has suggested to me that, had '*suco*' – an image introduced by Dante presumably partly to extend the line and preserve his rhyme-scheme – been understood by Mandelshtam as 'sap' or 'vital fluid' or 'essence', 'pith', 'heart' or 'gist' rather than as 'juice', his possibly confusing 'sponge' or 'rag' could have been avoided. *Premere* means to press; figuratively, to urge or insist upon. So the line, mistranslated by Mandelshtam, really means: I would urge (or stress or press) the gist of my conception. 'I find it ironic,' writes Holmes, 'that in this very line – *Io premerei di mio concetto il suco* – the terza rima *form* influences the form of words which influences (obfuscates?) the content-conception of the line itself.'

In a novel by Yury Koginov, the protagonist, referring to Tyutchev's poems, says that 'form' is like a glove, the form being

16

shaped by the hand ('content'); that in the best poetry, however, the form is more like the *skin* of the hand: skin and hand form one inseparable organic whole. Or, as Jennifer Baines has put it: 'Mandelshtam was tireless in his condemnation of those who advocated the separation of form from content.'*

Kiril Taranovsky, Nils Nilsson and Omry Ronen have in recent years addressed themselves to the question formulated by Akhmatova – 'who will tell us where that new, divine harmony, Mandelshtam's poetry, came from?' Thanks to their work (see Further Reading), we know much more about Mandelshtam's literary sub-texts and contexts, and about the 'echoes and correspondences, reflections and refractions' which Henry Gifford alludes to in an essay on Mandelshtam and Dante,† and are better able to decipher the message of Mandelshtam's texts.

The Russian text I have mostly used, and the numbering of Mandelshtam's poems given in brackets at the bottom of each poem, come from his *Sobraniye Sochineniy* (Collected Works), second edition revised and expanded, edited by G. P. Struve and B. A. Filippov, Inter-Language Literary Associates, Vol. I, Washington, 1967. Rather more than fifty of the poems contained in the present selection were not among those translated by Clarence Brown and W. S. Merwin in *Osip Mandelshtam; Selected Poems* (Oxford University Press, 1973; Penguin, 1977).

The Soviet editions of 1973 and 1974, edited by N. I. Khardzhiev, are not as comprehensive as the American edition. Of the poems translated here the Soviet editions exclude (in addition to both Odes to Stalin, positive and negative) nos 91, 165, 223, 233, 267/268, 307, 316, 318, 319, 320, 329, 341, 350, 351, 352, 353, 359, 368, 372, 380, 385 and 387, some for what must be ideological reasons.

In the following lines written as a black joke in 1935, Mandelshtam indicated what his official fate would be:

> What street's this one?
> – 'This is Mandelshtam Street.
> His disposition wasn't "party-line"
> Or "sweet-as-a-flower".
> That's why this street –
> Or, rather, sewer
> Or possibly slum –
> Has been named after
> Osip Mandelshtam.'

* *Mandelshtam: The Later Poetry*, 1976.

† *Dante and the Modern Poet, PN Review* 12, Vol. 6 No. 4.

After Stalin's death Mandelshtam was 'rehabilitated', but there is still no street anywhere in the Soviet Union named after him.

Mandelshtam's Voronezh poems of 1937 appear in this book in a new order. This is the result of Jennifer Baines's authoritative commentary, *Mandelshtam: The Later Poetry* (1976). Her dating, which is based on Nadezhda Yakovlevna Mandelshtam's own typescript copy of Mandelshtam's poems, is definitive and supersedes that of Struve and Filippov's American edition (but the numbering of the poems printed here is still Struve and Filippov's).

Many of the hundred-and-three translations in this volume are based on earlier versions contained in a selection first published by Elek Books in 1977, and reissued with additions and revisions by Granada Publishing in 1980. The poems I retain have all been revised, often radically, to keep pace with my understanding of Mandelshtam and to achieve a more precise relationship to the originals.

Eight poems from the 1980 volume have been liquidated: Nos 66, 84, 235, 275-85, 346/347, 357, 362, 374. The following are added to the present selection: Nos 62, 109, 140, 164, 222, 223, 233, 258, 267/268, 286, a passage from *Journey to Armenia*, 296, 299, 306, 312, 316, 318, 319, 320, part of the Ode to Stalin, 360.

Some of the earlier versions first appeared in *Agenda, Bananas, Cyphers, English, The New Review, New Statesman, The New Yorker, Poetry and Audience, Quarto, The Times Literary Supplement* and *Willow Springs*; and some were used in Caspar Wrede's play about Mandelshtam, *Hope against Hope*, put on at the Royal Exchange Theatre, Manchester in 1982.

I want to thank Donald Rayfield for contributing an introduction and select bibliography; and Mr N. Struve, of Editions YMCA-Press, Paris for permission to reprint the original Russian texts.

I am grateful to Antony Wood, without whose interest, patience and persistence this book might not have been published. I am also indebted to David Black, Robert Chandler, Eugene Dubnov, R. F. Holmes and Hugo Williams, and to Colette Ritchie for her typing.

Osip Mandelshtam: An Introduction

Born in 1891, Mandelshtam came early enough into Russian literature to be formed by the cultural surge of the 1900s known as the Silver Age. His father, an unprosperous leather merchant, was a Latvian Jew whose written language was German; his mother, from Vilno, was Russified in speech and outlook: 'Was she not the first of her whole family,' wrote her son, 'to achieve pure and clear Russian sounds?' Mandelshtam's first years were spent in Riga and Warsaw. A decade earlier he might have become a Yiddish, German or Polish poet, but in the 1900s discrimination in Russia was breaking down and Jews who were Russian citizens began to feel the Russian language to be their natural means of expression.

Jewish infancy was overlaid by a childhood spent in St Petersburg, and the education he received at the Tenishevsky school (where Vladimir Nabokov was to study) helped to make him a complete Hellene and European. His first lyrics show a passive receptiveness to the Symbolist other-worldliness typical of the times: Mandelshtam's receptiveness grew into a thirst for universal culture once he had spent several terms listening to Henri Bergson at the Sorbonne and studying at Heidelberg from 1907 to 1909. From now on he was convinced that the poet's immortal creation far outweighed in importance his mortal life: 'Condensation may vanish without trace,/But the cherished pattern no one can efface.'

Mandelshtam's views on culture and the poet's vocation were much influenced by the poet and poet's mentor Vyacheslav Ivanov (1866 – 1949), whose dualities of Dionysian disorder and Apollonic order became the energising polarities in Mandelshtam's thought, like the contrast of negative Judaic and positive Hellene, or Henri Bergson's objective and subjective time. Equally important was Mandelshtam's encounter with another great Symbolist, Innokenty Annensky (1856 – 1909), headmaster of the Tsarskoye Selo lyceum (the Eton of Russia). Annensky was a decadent poet of almost pathological modesty, who likewise saw European and Russian culture as indissolubly linked to ancient Greece, a balancing act between orderly art and chaotic numinous forces. Annensky, as translator and disciple of Verlaine, Rimbaud and Euripides, inculcated a respect for language and poetic responsibility.

Meeting Annensky's pupil, Nikolay Gumilev, was even more crucial for Mandelshtam's future: Mandelshtam, Gumilev and the latter's wife, the charismatic poet Anna Akhmatova, formed the core of a new poetic grouping which formally declared itself in 1913 to be the Acmeists. The word and the ideology are in themselves insignificant: Acmeism was to be for the rest of these poets' lives 'a yearning for world culture', a sense of the priority of poetic tradition over individual lyrical ego, a reaction against the worst of Symbolism – its pursuit of the occult, of empty musicality, its cult of decadent autobiography. Although Gumilev was shot in 1921 and Akhmatova spent most of her life many hundreds of miles away, Mandelshtam always felt them to be addressees and collocutors.

Mandelshtam never renounced Symbolism: in *Silentium* he gave priority to the idea over the reality: 'Remain as spray, Aphrodite,/ And – word – return to music . . .' But his early poetry that was to be published in 1913 as *Stone* turns more and more to symmetry, affirming architectural principles not only as the criteria for lasting poetry, but as the means of surmounting the poet's own personal inadequacy. Notre Dame cathedral is seen to unite the negative and positive, Northern chaos and Mediterranean order in European culture, 'The Gothic soul's rational abyss,/Egyptian power with Christian shyness', and inspires him to declare: 'I too one day shall create/Beauty from cruel weight.'

The Acmeists, like the Bolshevik conspirators calling themselves 'hammer', 'steel' and 'stone' – Molotov, Stalin, Kamenev – stressed the positive with their 'hard' titles: Mandelshtam's 'Stone' matches Gumilev's 'Pearls', Akhmatova's 'Beads', Zenkevich's 'Porphyry', in tribute to Théophile Gautier's 'Émaux et Camées'. But their greatness lay in their 'softness', the vulnerable, tragic side that eventually breaks through. In Mandelshtam, the victim and exile are never utterly silenced: if not 'Joseph, sold into Egypt', then Ovid (exiled to the Black Sea steppes, like Pushkin and eventually Mandelshtam) is an ominous precursor. Ovid was to give Mandelshtam the title of his second book, *Tristia*, in 1922: but in 'Horses' hooves . . .' of 1914 the poet already acknowledges him as the poet who 'sang of the ox- and bullock-waggons/In the march of the barbarians.'

Unlike the other Acmeists, but like their French counterparts such as Paul Valéry and Jean Moréas, Mandelshtam had by 1912 become a neo-classicist, reinterpreting the Mediterranean world as a timeless imaginary resource: the greatest poems of *Stone*, such as *The casino*, 'Golden orioles . . .', 'Sleeplessness. Homer. Stretched sail', merge the poet's mind with Homeric epic and Anacreontic idyll, so that the word becomes a world in itself: 'Golden orioles are in the woods, and length of vowels/Is the sole measure in accentual verse.' Time is bridged and the Hellenic world with its insecurity, an island surrounded by barbarians, undermined by Hades, is an analogue of the present: 'Homer speaks silently./And the black sea, thunderous orator,/Breaks on my pillow with a roar.'

By 1913, Mandelshtam was an original thinker as well as a mature poet. What is implicit in his poetics – the poet's ability to bridge time, to recreate past experiences in new languages – was made explicit in a daring series of intellectual forays. His essay on François Villon establishes a model for the poet as victim of the state; another essay, *On The Addressee,* makes imaginary conversation the basis of poetry; an essay on the first Russian thinker of note, the historiosopher Pyotr Chaadayev, argues the cyclic nature of history, for the need to interpret present experience as recognition of the past. These essays establish the role of the poet in history; they insist on continuity, on poetic language as a universal means of expression, constantly refined: they make Mandelshtam a proponent of Neo-classicism. which is to infuse and deepen his poetry for another twenty-five years, to an extent matched only in the work of T. S. Eliot.

The classical emphasis in Mandelshtam's *Stone* marked him apart from his fellow Acmeists: his lyrics have none of the egocentric, biographical core that we find in the best and worst of Gumilev and Akhmatova. Mandelshtam was even further in spirit and language from the Symbolists, whether the imprecise musicality of Blok or the occult rhetoric of Andrey Bely, while the dynamic barbarism of the Futurists, such as Khlebnikov and Mayakovsky, who were now denouncing European tradition in favour of experimental, aggressive poetics, could not have been more alien to him. Like Khodasevich, Mandelshtam had to wait for recognition simply because poets who were out to shock by self-dramatisation or provocative manifestos drew more critical fire.

The outbreak of war brought unexpected roles to the Acmeists. Very few Russian poets, however, took refuge in patriotic self-immolation: Gumilev was virtually the only poet to expose himself to front-line bullets. The Acmeists were too heavily committed to a united European culture to feel anything but horror at the disintegration of centuries-old contours and unities. The omens of 1914 and 1915, the smouldering peat-bogs around Petrograd (as St Petersburg became), the death of Russia's first

21

challenger to Beethoven, Skryabin, seemed harbingers of an apocalypse; fire, the extinction of the sun and of genius. Rachel's shattering performance in Petrograd of Racine's *Phèdre* left a deep impression, as though not just a mythological queen, but a sun goddess and an entire culture were perishing. Premonitions turned Akhmatova into a Cassandra, made even the warrior Gumilev into a 'poète maudit' and gave the last poems of Mandelshtam's *Stone* an insight into historical necessity which made him from now on the most contemporary and, in the deepest sense, the most political poet in Russia.

Like Mayakovsky, Khlebnikov, Blok and almost every Russian poet liable for service, Mandelshtam got exemption from the army. His perambulations over Russia and her Black Sea territories began: a brief affair with Marina Tsvetayeva led him to the Crimea, the setting for much of his later poetry, Russia's only overlap with the ancient Hellenic world, and then to Moscow, which Mandelshtam, like Baratynsky a hundred years before him, could not help fearing as a threateningly mediaeval Asiatic world. The disasters of war and the outbreak of revolution, culminating in the irreversible October 1917, drove him not only to flight but to acts and words of desperate heroism: his protests to the head of the Cheka, Dzerzhinsky, against arbitrary terror, his willingness to collaborate in the highest sense, but not in the lower, with such amenable Bolsheviks as Lunacharsky and Bukharin, match the poems of his that greet the revolution as the 'twilight of freedom', 'the unbearable weight of power'. He not only mourns, but interprets and admonishes.

Mandelshtam begins to detect cycles in Russian poetry, too: the events of 1917 and 1918 lead him back to his precursors in the eighteenth century. Marina Tsvetayeva had acclaimed him as a 'young Derzhavin': he follows Derzhavin in his treatment of the dying Petrograd as a city about to pass into Elysium, 'transparent Petropolis,/Where Proserpina rules over us.' The poetry of *Tristia* aligns with the Petersburg themes of doom so powerfully stated in Pushkin's *Bronze Horseman* and in Dostoevsky's novels; only now Mandelshtam has allied them to imagery of the black sun that pevades French tradition, from the lines he attributes to Phèdre, 'With my black love I have sullied the sun', to Nerval's 'Soleil noir de la mélancolie.'

He was never again allowed by fate or the authorities to re-establish himself in Petrograd/Leningrad: for the rest of his life it remained what Rome was to Ovid, a dying homeland, the centre of a lost empire. Mandelshtam never proclaimed allegiance to a new proletariat order; he refused to redirect his poetry to the masses; his peregrinations during the revolution to the Crimea under the Whites or Georgia under the Mensheviks were suspect; his loyalties to poets executed, like Gumilev, or exiled, like Vyacheslav Ivanov, condemned him to homelessness and eventually exile. In the eyes of the Soviet establishment he was a shadowy, even a shady figure: and the frequency of the word *ten'*, shade, shadow, in his poetry must be significant.

The Crimea, where Mandelshtam like so many Russian writers fled for warmth and food, became a fragile dreamworld. Here the White armies hung on until 1921 and it was possible to drink milk and honey, to relegate the reality of the north to the status of a recurrent nightmare. The title poem and the central poems of *Tristia* oppose a carefully nurtured Hellenic dreamworld of sensuality to a threatening outside temporal force: these poems reenact an opposition between internal time (in Russian, *vek*) and external time (*vremya*), very like the contrast we find in another assimilated Jew, Marcel Proust.

The sensuality of *Tristia* gives Mandelshtam's love poetry an almost palpable sonority: in 1919, he met Nadezhda Khazina; in 1921 he married her and a life-long dependence began, surviving his periodic infatuations which inspired some of the richest love poetry in the language. Like Catullus, whom Mandelshtam had studied very closely (despite failing his Latin examinations at university), he is moved by love when most threatened by death. The poem *Tristia* deals with the pain of separation from physical love, from life and from inspiration and from a culture as though they were all variants of one 'science of goodbyes'. It is the culmination of the Russian elegy, which amounts to the major lyrical genre of the language, celebrating loss not merely of life, but of love and language. Thus the first stanza's 'bareheaded laments at night' are linked to the political betrayal implicit in the 'cock's clamour' of the second stanza and the poetic frustration – 'How threadbare the language of happiness' – in the third stanza. After linking all three levels of experience – amatory, political and poetic – as firmly as Ovid ever had, Mandelshtam is able to draw the first of a number of statements on the separate role of men and women in tragic times. 'Wax is for women what bronze is for men,' he concludes, an idea which grows out of the different roles of himself as a victim and Akhmatova as a survivor, both Cassandra and Antigone, and amounts to a completely classical tragic philosophy. It holds true until the year before his death, when he addresses his young friend Natasha

Shtempel with an almost unbearable summons: 'There are women who are natives of the sodden earth:/Their every step a hollow sobbing,/Their calling to accompany the dead.'

The Neo-classical craftmanship of *Tristia* was greeted by sympathetic critics as 'the overcoming of Symbolism'; in fact, *Tristia*'s precision of tone is a preparation for the more starkly expressed revelations of the poetry of the 1930s. In 1922, however, Mandelshtam's achievement was more noticeable than a decade earlier: the Symbolists had died, emigrated or abandoned poetry; surviving Futurists, such as Mayakovsky, had lapsed for a while into versifying propaganda; the new proletarian poets were disappointing in their incompetence. Only Pasternak's *My Sister Life* – 'a cure for tuberculosis' as Mandelshtam generously acclaimed it – made a greater impact than *Tristia*, for Pasternak flooded his readers with sense impressions, private allusions and breathless inventiveness, quite unlike the orderly Hellenic imagery, the elegiac cadences and traditional sonorities of Mandelshtam. Before his execution, Gumilev had become disorientated enough to develop into a Symbolist; Akhmatova, on the verge of silence, had reduced poetry to austere aphorism: Mandelshtam was the only recognisable major Acmeist poet still writing.

Eventually, he made his way back from the Hellenic hinterland to Moscow, travelling over the Black Sea to Georgia three times between 1919 and 1922. Unlike Pasternak and Zabolotsky, however, he was never able to establish himself in the more hospitable Caucasus; too unsettled and outspoken to fit in with the ritual respect offered to poets, too preoccupied with the need to confront the moral vacuum at the centre of power, he returned to Petrograd and Moscow.

The proof that Mandelshtam was political is to be found in his heroic protests to Dzerzhinsky and Bukharin about Blyumkin, a secret-policeman whom he caught filling in a blank signed death-warrant with innocent names: this act put Mandelshtam's life at risk and may have contributed to his final doom. More important still are his much misinterpreted 'historiosophic' poems, such as *The Twilight of Freedom*, where the revolution is seen as a cosmic catastrophe, the earth out of its orbit, and the poet reacts with sympathy, not condemnation, for the leaders attempting to take the helm. Like Blok's *The Twelve*, such poems were misunderstood and condemned by left and right: the left could not forgive the elegiac tone and the right could not share the sense of tragic necessity. Those Bolsheviks, such as Lunacharsky and Bukharin, who could value such interpretations of their revolution, were few and very vulnerable. The real menace of the times was brought home to Mandelshtam in 1921 by the execution of Gumilev which, for all its self-willed martyrdom, was the first of several events that shifted Mandelshtam's allegiance to the world of the dead.

The world of the dead is ever-present in *Tristia*: Mandelshtam is constantly trying to retrieve his thoughts from the shadowy realm of Persephone, the refuge of Psyche, who symbolises for him the free spirit, the unspoken word. 'The blind swallow flies back to her palace of shadows./Night songs are sung in frenzied absentmindedness.' Swallows, the classical symbol of communication between the land of the living and the city of the dead, represent both free poetic thought and political freedom to Mandelshtam: the coming of totalitarianism he imagines as the 'binding of swallows into battle legions'. His poetics and his historical thinking are indivisible.

Mandelshtam's long-term view was perhaps even less acceptable to Soviet ideology than Gumilev's straightforward hostility. After *Tristia* Mandelshtam found his access to publishers more and more difficult. His attempts to settle in Leningrad foundered on hostility and he was forced by 1928 to settle in Moscow. The last poems of *Tristia* date from 1921: in any case the atmosphere for lyrical poetry was growing too rare. Russian literature felt itself to have reached an epic phase, where only narrative prose and the cinema could hope to assimilate what had happened. From 1922, Akhmatova and Pasternak virtually deserted lyricism for other fields, Akhmatova for the 'genre of silence', Pasternak for the illusive objectivity of narrative poetry, and Mandelshtam likewise moved towards prose as self-expression and translation as a means of earning a living. The Soviet reader naturally benefited from the influx of talent in translation and children's books, written by those who were refugees from their own thoughts, but the history of Russian poetry came to a decade or so's hiatus in 1923.

The 'other voice of prose' which Mandelshtam revealed in the mid-1920s was no mere surrogate, but an equally penetrating and perhaps even more original alternative to verse. The 'anti-memoirs' of *The Noise of Time* are a haunting evocation of the cultural influences – texts, teachers, childhood friends – on the adolescent poet, and the novella *The Egyptian Stamp* is a dense hallucinatory vision of the revolution and its effect on the naive poetic persona. (Both works have been translated by Clarence Brown.) But this is more than autobiography, fictionalised or not: 'I want to speak about something other than myself, to follow the age, the noise and

25

growth of time . . . Revolution is itself life and death and cannot bear hearing people trivialising life and death. Its throat is dry with thirst but it will not accept a single drop of moisture from an outsider's hands.' But for all its importance as a vehicle for tracing his spiritual growth and measuring his distance and involvement, Mandelshtam, unlike Pasternak, never allowed prose to supplant verse. For a few years his poetry was undergoing a period of pupation before it burst out, metamorphosed and not immediately recognisable.

The relatively few poems of 1921 to 1924 lie halfway between the musicality of *Tristia* and the silence of the later 20s: one's first reaction is to dismiss them as cryptic. But a reading of earlier Mandelshtam makes deciphering straightforward: the difference is that these are written for a familiar reader, who has mastered the code for his images' symbolic values. The density of 'I was washing at night in the courtyard,' which sets with minimal text a starlit night reflected in a rainwater butt, expands into sense when we remember the value of starlight as unalterable truth, salt as an image of painful realisation, so that the eight-line poem becomes a cosmic contrast of eternal clarity and temporary murk, as stark and unmusical as a mathematical equation.

The compression of Mandelshtam's ideas of private and public time is most powerful in *My Time* of 1923, where time is seen as a beast with a broken spine, turned cruel and vindictive, the poet unable to restore its unity. Here Mandelshtam has compressed an idea that goes back through Mayakovsky and Cubist painting to Verlaine, the idea of a whole human-being as a musical instrument (the flute as the image of the spine, the vertebrae its keys), whose only purpose is harmony and which is destroyed when its integrity is broken: Verlaine's *Art Poétique* and Mayakovsky's *Flute-Spine* are subsumed here, as is the classical tradition of Russian poetry, Pushkin and Tyutchev, in the vision of nature still 'gushing out greenly' while human life is crushed to death.

Before his six years' silence, Mandelshtam also experimented with freer, more expansive forms, explicitly or implicitly odes, to deal with the vast disparities between an increasingly threatening Moscow and the starry eternity by which he had always measured events and time. Political imagery gives way to metaphors of predation, oppression and summary execution, traditional in Russian fable and urban folklore: *1st January 1924* has imagery of judicial murder: 'lips sealed with tin', the Underwood typewriter with the cartilage of a pike and deadly 'layers of lime'. The imagery of threat and the astral symbols lie dormant until they surface with renewed effect in the 1930s. These six years, however unhappy in their wanderings and insecurity, were not entirely wasted. Like other Acmeists, Mandelshtam sought refuge in new spheres of activity, notably in reading and translating Italian poetry, which seemed to hold the secret of survival in an age of lethal political conflict. Dante and Petrarch were soon to be of enormous significance to Mandelshtam as sources of themes, even new sounds, but above all as mapmakers of hell.

Hostility and suspicion in literary circles, even from such established pre-revolutionary figures as Andrey Bely, drove Mandelshtam into new intellectual regions. In the Soviet Union speculation was still relatively free among natural and physical scientists: the biologists and physicists so valuable to the Communists' development plans were the last reservoir of free thinking and international communication. It was among them that Mandelshtam found new acquaintance and ideas. Not until the 1930s were these new themes assimilated into Mandelshtam's poetics, but they were to give his poetry, and that of his younger contemporary Zabolotsky, resources almost unprecedented in European literature.

Even in *My Time* of 1923, Mandelshtam shows an impressive familiarity with biological terminology; biology is the first of the sciences – followed by physics and cosmology – to enlarge his poetics. By 1930 he had made friends with Boris Kuzin, an eager proponent of neo-Lamarckism, a theory of evolution discredited before and since which propounds the inheritance of acquired characteristics and supposes that species evolve by an almost spiritual response to the demands of their environment. Stalin and his charlatan agronomist Lysenko favoured this pre-Darwinian theory for its implications in creating *homo sovieticus* out of *homo sapiens* and for the promise of training wheat to grow in the Arctic: very soon, however, the neo-Lamarckists were to be purged for the implicit idealism, even theism, of their doctrines. Mandelshtam went back to the original *Philosophie zoologique* of 1809 and saw something the biologists had ignored: Lamarck treats evolution as though it were literally a descent from warm-blooded humanity through the reptiles to the insensate protean forms of life and implies, as well he might after his bitter experience of the French revolution, that evolution is a reversible process, a ladder (*une échelle*) that nature could well descend or even snatch away. Furthermore, Lamarck's hierarchical survey of the genera and families of animals uncannily echoes Dante's nine circles of hell, each circle blacker and more painful.

Biology and Italian poetry are linked: the narrative thread spun

27

by Ariosto in the poem of that name, the cult of the dead Laura in the Petrarch sonnets that Mandelshtam so lovingly translated in 1933, the yearning for an unattainable Florence and Tuscany in the poems of the 1930s all correspond to Lamarck's exploration of nature's abysses, the unattainable sixth sense in 'the lizard's pineal eye' (the 4th eight-line poem of 1934): these are secret worlds: as a variant of *Ariosto* puts it, 'Friend of Ariosto, Petrarch and Tasso – /Senseless, salty-sweet language/And the charming bivalves of clinched sounds, – /I'm afraid to open the clam's pearl with a knife.' Their labyrinthine symmetry creates a structure that enables Mandelshtam to make tragic sense of Stalin's epoch.

This relevance of the Italian classics and of natural sciences to his predicament struck Mandelshtam on his last journey into Asia, a trip with biologists to Armenia that Bukharin's patronage had gained for him. The 1930s brought about the 'impact of Asia' on Mandelshtam and many of his contemporaries: for Russian poets, Armenia and Georgia had replaced Italy and France as lands where lemon trees bloomed. Given the traditional Russian associations of Asia with the blind tyranny of Medes and Persians as opposed to Europe's Hellenic freedom, it is only natural that Soviet poets should see ominous relevance in the cultural switch they were forced to make that accords with MacNeice's lines: 'For we are obsolete who like the lesser things,/Who play in corners with looking-glass and beads;/It is better we should go quickly, go into Asia . . .'

Dante, biology and Asia were the explosive: the detonator was provided by the second important death in Mandelshtam's career, that of Mayakovsky, which 'released the stream of poetry' in him, as his widow phrased it. If Mayakovsky, sympathiser and propagandist, could not live under the regime, then the 'genre of silence' appeared to offer no safeguards. However irrational the reasoning, both Pasternak and Mandelshtam experienced a 'second birth' on Mayakovsky's death: between 1930 and 1932 they wrote what are arguably their finest and boldest lyrics, using the last bubbles of freedom and the incomprehension of their censors to get them into print, before twenty years of terror took poetry back to a purely oral genre.

In Tbilisi, on his way back from Armenia, in November 1930 Mandelshtam wrote a remarkable chain of stanzas to celebrate his reawakening to new, harsher textures, a 'cat language' of oral and written scratches and an Asiatic endurance of history's oppression. Years later, when Armenia has faded from his themes, the new sensations of being blinded and deafened by menacing colours and sounds are permanently incorporated into Mandelshtam's phonetic line and images. Armenia thus gives Mandelshtam not just a landscape for a new era – 'a costly clay' – but a new Asiatic language, rich in whispered consonants, fit for *sotto voce* and hermetic writing. But its history, the fall of a kingdom to imperial tyranny, is of allegorical importance in the prose account Mandelshtam wrote of his Journey. This poetic prose mingles history, landscape and travelogue with an account of Mandelshtam's induction into science, 'Around the Naturalists', and eventually gives rise to poems such as *Lamarck* of 1932 in which he identifies with the neglected 'patriarch' of evolution and prepares to experience his descent into the world of the arachnids, a typically spidery hell for Russian writers.

Between 1932 and his first arrest in 1934 Mandelshtam treats Russian, Italian and German poets in the same way as he does Lamarck, as precursors whom he must follow to the bitter end, whether the deviously self-sustaining narration of Ariosto or the arrogance of Pushkin's predecessor, Batyushkov, who pursued his 'eternal dreams, samples of blood,/From one glass to another' at the cost of his own sanity. Alien tongues are not just sources of new ideas, material for translation but – as Latin and Greek had been in the 1920s and 1920s – means for personal survival. Addressing the heroic *Sturm und Drang* poets in *To the German Language*, Mandelshtam declares that 'An alien language will be a foetal membrane for me,/And long before I dared be born.'

Literary survival, however, was harder: the editor who published the *Journey to Armenia* was lucky to lose merely his job. Mandelshtam had enormous difficulty finding the meanest housing, was provoked by attacks and accusations into leaving the newly formed Union of Writers, and was barred from publication. Then with suicidal spirit he composed a lampoon on Stalin – a talent for satirical verse had made him a successful children's versifier – and no one could save him. Stalin, who had himself been a Romantic poet in Georgia as an adolescent, took a close and deadly interest in Russian poetry: he would have been unlikely to forgive Mandelshtam's allusiveness, and the lines on 'His fat fingers slimy as worms', for all the acknowledgement of his power ('He forges his decrees like horseshoes'), were an eventual death warrant.

The intervention of Pasternak and Bukharin reprieved Mandelshtam he was sent to a remote town in the Urals and after a suicide attempt was allowed to choose the steppe town of Voronezh for three years' exile. But his mental and physical health was broken and after the first wave of purges began in 1934 it was clear that this first arrest was only the prelude to a second and final blow.

For thirty years it was assumed that Mandelshtam had been destroyed as a poet: it was natural that, like almost everyone else, he should be silenced by fear if not by depression. Only after 1961, when his widow and the others who had stood by him – Akhmatova and Natasha Shtempel – released the manuscripts they had preserved in pillowcases and saucepans or reconstructed from memory and scraps of paper, did it become clear that there was a posthumous Mandelshtam, at first barely compatible with the known poet, to be disinterred from Voronezh. Slowly the poems have emerged in the Soviet Union, in *Literary Georgia* or *Questions of Linguistics*, and quickly they amassed in the West. Despite the loss of Mandelshtam's original manuscripts, the theft and destruction of much of his archive by self-appointed trustees or the NKVD, enough friends committed them to paper or memory for us to be sure that the versions now in print are as good as originals. (Many are variants, but as the notebooks were not fully prepared for publication we cannot always say whether one version of a poem supersedes another.) The Voronezh poems amount to a quarter of Mandelshtam's work and are arguably his finest. It has taken time for those who love the measured sonority of the early work to come to terms with the sometimes harsh, nervous and very dense language of the later work, and for the continuity between the two to become apparent.

What are now known as the Voronezh notebooks are 189 pages spanning three years: they represent three intense spurts spaced by long months of almost total silence: 23 poems date from spring and summer 1935; the second notebook's fifty poems come from nine weeks of the winter of 1936/7, while the last notebook holds about two dozen poems from spring 1937. The poems are precisely dated and show some thematic grouping: the first volume of Nadezhda Yakovlevna's memoirs, *Hope against Hope*, should be read for the evidence of their authenticity and their origin.

The first notebook has to cope with a new landscape – the forests of the Urals and the black earth of the steppe so alien to Mandelshtam's urban or Hellenic scenery. Drawing on the phrase of Voronezh's famous nineteenth-century pseudo-folk poet Koltsov – 'step-mother steppe' (a pun in English, not in Russian) – , Mandelshtam makes literal his own image of poetry as a plough digging up time, ('. . . the earth ploughs the ear with a chilly, morning clarinet') and arrives at a surrogate of the musicality he needs in his surroundings: 'a mildewed flute'. That sense of a ruined instrument stays with his Voronezh poetry, culminating in the 'Greek flute' that slips from the poet's hands and lips in 1937. Far from the sea that moulded St Petersburg and the Crimea, Mandelshtam feels his new element, the black earth, to be fit only for the burial of 'This vertebral, charred flesh'.

A little work for radio in 1935, a sanatorium stay in Tambov, a visit by Anna Akhmatova, support from Pasternak and from Natasha Shtempel (who risked her own and her family's lives to befriend the Mandelshtams) enabled the poet, despite the new wave of purges sweeping the country, to gather his strength for the extraordinarily productive few months of the second and third Voronezh notebooks, in which all his interests, imagery and linguistic resources combined. Modern physics and Christianity he had already discovered to be linked in the work of Pavel Florensky, priest and mathematician, who proved that Dante's cosmology could only be reconciled with Einstein's theory of relativity: this stimulates Mandelshtam to new syntheses. Writing his *Conversation about Dante*, he treats himself as an explorer of hell, and he learns to face Christian demonology in the steppes. His lines, 'What can we do with the murderous plains?/. . . And is not he who makes us, sleeping, shriek/Slowly crawling across them – /The Judas of all future men?', sound the same apocalyptic alarm as Yeats' 'rough beast . . . slouching towards Bethlehem to be born.'

Like every interpreter of the apocalypse, Mandelshtam begins to detect ominous parallels. His verse had always invested much of its power in rhyme, in the significance of assonance. In the poems of the second Voronezh notebook, coincidences of sound between opposites take on extraordinary meaning. The whispering 'cat language' – *k, p, t, ch* – of Armenian is combined with rich earthy sounds – *or, ar*; traditional Russian puns, such as the rhyme of *guby*, lips, with *gubit'*, to destroy, are enlarged. Words such as *os'*, axis, become crucial, since they link the poet (*Osip*) with his persecutor, *Josef* Stalin, and negative images such as wasps (*osy*). The weft is so elaborate that Mandelshtam now begins to defy translation.

A full understanding of this poetry is perhaps unattainable, even with the help of Nadezhda's memoirs, so varied and often private are the sources and references: Voronezh's art gallery, chance remarks by visitors as well as new reading merge with Mandelshtam's rekindled sense of his own Jewishness: 'I'm plunged into a lion's den/. . . Under the yeast shower of these sounds:/. . . more potent that the Pentateuch.' Only in 1987, for instance, have

Natasha Shtempel's memoirs been published and the dedicatory import of many poems, such as 'With her irregular delightful way of walking', been confirmed.

One clear development links the fate of the cosmos, the starry firmament, to that of the human skull, both vaults, repositories of truth now vulnerable to extinction. Poem after poem connects the movement of the human face, e.g. *The Birth of a Smile*, with the creation of order out of chaos, 'A rainbow ties them both together,/A glimmer of Atlantis strikes both eyes', so that imagery of doom latent in the tender infant's cartilage and the lost city of Atlantis coexist with the affirmation of creation. Mandelshtam, at his serenest, achieves a Lamarckian acceptance that the 'escalator' of evolution has to go into reverse. Just as women's role is to mourn men, so the male poet's role is to mourn the universe: poetry remains for him what it always was – elegy. 'And I have accompanied the rapture of the universe/As muted organ pipes/Accompany a woman's voice.'

Serenity did not silence protest: by the end of February 1937, Mandelshtam's longest and most devious poem was finished: *Verses on the unknown Soldier*. The title clearly destined it for publication: the naive could read it as a lament for the victims of the First World War, as today the Soviet editors introduce it as a prophecy of the Second. It is only too obviously a lament for the still unsung victims of the purges, and ends with a cry of fear. But the most frightening aspect of the poem is its incorporation of modern quantum physics and astronomy (a subject on which Mandelshtam's namesake was then lecturing in Moscow university) and the anticipation of ideas yet to be born: the universe seen as a 'black oyster' in which starlight, once the source and image-bearer of ineradicable truths, is to be swallowed up. The starry vault whose image the human skull reflects is about to collapse. In this sense Stalin is a Copernicus capable of destroying cosmic harmony.

Mandelshtam redirected his attention to Stalin, forcing himself to the act of degradation inflicted on almost every poet, doomed or saved, in the 1930s: an ode to Stalin. But, incapable of simulation, he failed. Stalin appears as a counterpart to himself, the negative of the poet, sometimes through the same image, as an 'idol in a cave' surrounded by bones, trying 'to recollect his human guise'. Only in ambiguity could Mandelshtam attempt any conciliation. Like novelists such as Bulgakov and Zamyatin, he was interested in the mind and pathology of his enemy to the point of sympathy, but not of panegyric.

In April 1937, Mandelshtam was denounced as a Trotskyist: although his exile was coming to an end, he was living on borrowed time. That spring, inspired by the marriage of Natasha Shtempel as well as the suicides and disappearances in Voronezh, there is a final burst of lyricism, as though he were confident that the survival of his verse was assured. The influence of Keats (Nadezhda knew English poetry) seems to underlie his poems on the Cretan urns and the Greek flute, which stand for a continuous creative spirit that moves from one ephemeral vessel to another. The Greek flute commemorates not only a Voronezh musician who was purged, but the Hellenic creative spirit which the poet no longer has the strength to express: 'Squeezing clods of clay to death in my hands,/My measure has changed to disease.' The Russian language seems to prove the involvement of death in creation: *mor*, disease, links with *mera*, measure, just as the syllable *ub* is present in the words for lips, murder, diminish. The Greek *thalassa* and *thanatos*, sea and death, are the beginnings and endings of poetry, as their assonance shows.

Mandelshtam was virtually the only important Russian poet writing in the mid 1930s. The purges had silenced every major talent. Pasternak wrote his *Artist* in 1936 during a brief lull in the terror, but soon succumbed to the prevailing atmosphere; Nikolay Zabolotsky relied on his Aesopic, fauve technique to write about the disjointing of the times, while appearing to praise the brave new world around him, but the censors understood him and he was swept away in the same wave that destroyed Mandelshtam. Even abroad, poetic inspiration had apparently deserted Marina Tsvetaeva: Mandelshtam had no cultural milieu, no critical response, no publications after 1934 and even his private readers were too frightened to respond. The Voronezh poems were written for the poet and a shadowy posterity: the lack of feedback is one of the reasons for their nervous, cryptic and compressed tone.

Their exile officially expired, the Mandelshtams managed to spend only three days in Leningrad and Moscow: they found temporary shelter in Kalinin. Then in spring 1938, with suspicious ease, they were found a place in a country sanatorium: on 2 May, Osip Mandelshtam was arrested. The protectors of poets at the court of Stalin were soon themselves to face the firing squad: Mandelshtam was processed as a counter-revolutionary and, starved, perhaps deranged, died in a transit camp in far-eastern Siberia on 27 December 1938.

With extraordinary determination, like the women at the cross, Nadezhda, Natasha Shtempel and Anna Akhmatova ensured his resurrection and the eventual triumphant entry of his poetry into the Judaic and Hellenic tradition. At enormous risk they preserved what they could in the chaos of the war years and the repressive years of Stalin's senility. A very few Russian critics, such as Khardzhiev and Shklovsky, and a few intrepid foreign scholars ensured that Mandelshtam's name, by the mid 1960s, became known not only to two new generations of Russian readers, but to virtually the entire world. As James Greene and, before him, Paul Celan have shown, Mandelshtam's concern for precision, musicality and continuity make him one of the most translatable poets Russia has ever produced. In Russian poetry, his influence began in the 1960s: as a protégé of Anna Akhmatova, Joseph Brodsky became a vector of Mandelshtamian poetics for Russian poets. While we cannot say that a tradition of Jewish verse exists in Russia, Judaism, as Mandelshtam puts it, 'like a drop of musk filling a whole house', adds a tension and internationalism to a lyrical tradition which could not otherwise have survived the rarefaction of the atmosphere.

February 1988   *Donald Rayfield*

From STONE (1913, 1916, 1923 and 1928)

Fruit breaking loose from tree:
The cautious muffled sound,
Incessant singing
Of deep forest silence all around. . .

(1)   1908

You slipped out in a light shawl
From the dimly-lit hall;
The servants slept on,
We disturbed no one . . .

(3)   1908

To read only children's books,
To cherish child-like thoughts, to throw
Everything grown-up away,
To rise out of deep sorrow . . .

I'm tired to death of life,
I welcome nothing it can give me,
But I adore my naked earth:
There's no other one to see.

A simple wooden swing
And the darkness of the lofty fir
As I swung in a far-off garden,
I remember in a hazy fever.

(4)   1908

April-blue enamel:
Now conceivable, though pale,
At evening inconspicuously
Birch-trees hammock in the sky.

Fine netting cuts
Thin patterns exactly:
Designs on porcelain plates
Traced accurately

By a considerate artist
On his firmament of glass –
Knowing a short-lived strength,
Oblivious of sad death.

(6)   1909

What shall I do with the body I've been given,
So much at one with me, so much my own?

For the calm happiness of breathing, being able
To be alive, tell me to whom I should be grateful?

I'm gardener, flower too, and not alone
In the world's dungeon.

My warmth, my exhalation you can already see
On the window-pane of eternity.

A pattern is printed on it,
Unrecognisable until this minute.

Condensation may vanish without trace,
But the cherished pattern no one can efface.

(8)   1909

An inexpressible sadness
Opened two big eyes,
A vase of flowers woke up
And splashed its crystal.

The whole room was filled
With languor – that sweet medicine!
Such a small kingdom
To swallow so much sleep.

A little red wine,
A little sunlight in May –
And fine white fingers
Breaking a thin biscuit.

(9)   1909

Newly-reaped ears of early wheat
Lie in level rows;
Fingertips thrill and press against
Fingers fragile as themselves.

1909

Words are unnecessary,
There's nothing to impart,
And how sad and exemplary
An animal's dark heart!

It has no wish to be astounding,
It cannot use words:
Like a young dolphin sounding
The grey gulfs of worlds.

(11)   1909

Silentium

The breast of the sea heaves peacefully,
Like a lunatic the bright day sparkles,
And the spray is pale lilac
In a bowl of murky blue.

May my lips attain
Their original speechlessness,
A note high and clear,
Unsmirched by being born.

Remain as spray, Aphrodite,
And – word – return to music,
And – fused with life's foundation –
Heart, be ashamed of heart!

(14)   1910

The ear-drums stretch their sensitive sail,
Eyes – dilating – glaze,
An unsinging choir of midnight birds
Swims across the silence.

I am as poor as nature,
As naked as the sky,
And my freedom is spectral
Like the voice of the midnight birds.

I see the unbreathing moon
And a sky deader than canvas;
Your strange and morbid world
I welcome, emptiness!

(15)   1910

Like the shadow of sudden clouds,
A sea-guest staggers past
And, rippling by, sighs
Along embarrassed shores.

An enormous sail austerely soars;
Dead-white, the wave shrinks back –
And once more will not dare
To touch the shore;

And the boat, rustling through the waves . . .

(16)   1910

I grew out of a dangerous swamp,
Rustling like a reed,
And – with rapture, languor, caresses –
Inhale a prohibited life.

In my cold and marshy refuge
No one notices me,
And I'm welcomed by the whisper
Of short autumn minutes.

I enjoy this cruel injury;
And in a life like a dream
Secretly I envy everybody,
Secretly am in love with the world.

(17)   1910

Sultry dusk covers the couch,
I'm stifling . . .
Dearest of all to me, perhaps,
The delicate cross and secret path.

(19)   1910

How slowly the horses move,
How dark the light the lanterns throw!
Where they're taking me
These strange ones surely know.

I am cold, I want to sleep.
Confident of their concern,
Suddenly towards starlight
I'm thrown at the turn.

The nodding of a fevered head,
The caring icy hand of a stranger,
And – once more unseen by me –
Outlines of dark fir.

(20)   1911

Light sows a meagre beam
Coldly in the sodden forest.
I carry slowly in my heart
The grey bird, sadness.

What shall I do with the wounded bird?
The earth is effaced, silent, dead.
From a belfry masked by mist
Somebody stole the bells.

The high air stands
Dumb and bereaved,
A white and empty tower
Of quietness and mist.

The morning's tenderness – half real,
Half reverie – is never-ending.
Miracle of drowsiness and lull;
Mist-like thoughts are ringing . . .

(21)   1911

The sea-shell

It may be, night, you don't need me;
Out of the world's abyss,
Like a shell without pearls,
I'm hurled on your shores.

You stir the waves indifferently
And incorrigibly sing;
But you shall loyally esteem
This equivocal, unnecessary thing.

You lie down on the sand close by,
Wrap your chasuble around,
And indissolubly bind to the shell
The colossal bell of the waves.

The walls of the brittle shell,
Like a heart where no one lives,
Your whispering spray shall fill
With wind and rain and mist.

(26)   1911

I loathe the light
Of the monotonous stars . . .

Campanile! Lattice, be lace –
Become a cobweb, stone:
Lacerate the void
With your fine needle.

Either my turn shall come:
I sense the spreading of a wing;
But will my arrow wound
And animate?

Or, my time and journey over,
I shall return:
I couldn't love – there.
Here – I'm afraid to . . .

(*from* 29)   1912

In the haze your image
Trembled; it troubled
And eluded me:
'Good God!' I said, unthinkingly.

The name of the Lord – a large bird –
Flew out of my breast.
In front: a swirl of mist.
Behind: the empty cage.

(30)   1912

No, not the moon, but the bright clock-face
Shines on me. Am I to blame
If the feeble stars strike me as milky?

And I'm against the loftiness of Batyushkov.
When asked the time,
His answer was 'Eternity'.

(31)   1912

The one who walks

I'm conquered by dread
When faced with mysterious heights;
A swallow in the sky pleases me,
And I love the way a bell-tower soars!

I feel I am the age-old traveller
Who, on winding paths, above the precipice,
Listens to the snow-ball grow
And timelessness strike on clocks of stone.

If it could be! But I'm not that wayfarer
Flickering against faded foliage:
Genuine sadness sings in me.

There's an avalanche in the hills!
And all my self is in the bells,
Though music cannot save one from the abyss!

(32)   1912

The casino

I don't favour premeditated happiness.
Sometimes nature's a grey blemish
And I'm sentenced, slightly tipsy,
To taste the colours of a poor existence.

The wind is playing with a corrugated cloud,
The anchor scrapes the ocean bottom;
Lifeless as linen, my wine-struck mind
Hangs over nothingness.

But I revel in the casino on the dunes:
The vast view from the misty window,
A thin ray of light on the crumpled tablecloth;

And, when the wine is flashing in its crystal like a rose
And there's green water all around,
I like to soar – the grey gull's shadow!

(33)   1912

The Lutheran

On a walk, I met a funeral,
Near the Lutheran church last Sunday.
An absentminded passer-by, I stopped to watch,
Rigorous distress on the faces of the flock.

I couldn't make out what language they were speaking,
And nothing shone except gaunt bridles
And reflections from the lazy horse-shoes
On the toneless Sunday side-roads.

In the resilient half-light of the carriage
Where sadness, the dissembler, lay entombed,
Wordless and tearless and grudging greetings
A buttonhole of autumn roses gleamed.

Black-ribboned foreigners kept step
And ladies weak from weeping went on foot,
Red faces veiled, as obstinately, above,
The coachman drove straight on.

Whoever you are, Lutheran now deceased,
Your funeral rites were artlessly observed,
A decorous tear misted all eyes duly,
The bells rang out with dignified restraint.

I thought – no need to be rhetorical:
We're not prophets nor precursors,
We don't delight in heaven or live in fear of hell;
We burn, like candles, in dull noon.

(37)   1912

Hagia Sophia

Hagia Sophia – here the Lord commanded
That nations and tsars should halt!
Your dome, according to a witness,
Hangs from heaven by a chain.

All ages take their measure of Justinian:
Diana from her shrine in Ephesus allowed

One hundred and seven pillars of green marble
To be pillaged for his alien gods.

How did your bountiful builder feel
When – with lavish hand and lofty spirit –
He set the apses and the chapels,
Arranging them at east and west?

A splendid temple, bathing in the peace –
A festival of light from forty windows;
Under the dome, on pendentives, the four Archangels
Sail onwards, most beautiful of all.

And this sage and spherical building
Shall outlive nations and their centuries,
Nor shall the seraphs' resonant sobbing
Warp the dark gilt surfaces.

(38)   1912

Notre Dame

Where a Roman judged a foreign people
A basilica stands and, first and joyful
Like Adam once, an arch plays with its own ribs:
Groined, muscular, never-unnerved.

From outside, the bones betray the plan:
Flying buttresses proclaim
That cumbersome mass shall never ram the wall,
The onslaught of a crashing vault is hindered.

Elemental labyrinth, unfathomable forest,
The Gothic soul's rational abyss,
Egyptian power with Christian shyness,
Oak and reed – and perpendicular as tsar.

But the more attentively I studied,
Notre Dame, your monstrous ribs, your stronghold,
The more I thought: I too one day shall create
Beauty from cruel weight.

(39)   1912

Poisoned bread, and satiated air.
Wounds impossible to bind!
Joseph, sold into Egypt, couldn't have pined
With a more passionate despair!

Bedouin, under the starry sky,
Each on a horse,
Shut their eyes and improvise
Out of the troubles of the day gone by.

Images lie close at hand:
One traded horses,
Another lost his quiver in the sand.
The haze of happenings disperses.

If genuinely sung,
Wholeheartedly – at last
Nothing is left
But space, and stars, and song.

(54)   1913

Horses' hooves . . . The clatter
Of stark and simple times.
And the yardmen, in their sheepskin coats,
Sleep on the wooden benches.

A clamour at the iron gates
Wakes the royally-lazy doorman,
Whose wolf-like yawning
Recalls the brutal Scythians

When Ovid – his love now on the wane –
Blended Rome and snow,
And sang of the ox- and bullock-waggons
In the march of the barbarians.

(60)   1914

Golden orioles are in the woods, and length of vowels
Is the sole measure in accentual verse.
But only once a year is nature lengthily protracted
And overflowing, as in Homer's measure.

Today yawns like a caesura:
Quiet since morning, and arduous duration;
Oxen at pasture, and a golden indolence
To extract from the reed one whole note's richness.

(62)   1914

Nature is Roman, and mirrored in Rome.
We see its forms of civic grandeur
In transparent air, like a sky-blue circus,
Fields in the Forum and groves in colonnades.

Nature is Roman, and it seems
Vainglorious now to trouble any god:
There are sacrificial entrails to foretell war,
Slaves to be silent, stones to be built!

(65)   1914

Sleeplessness. Homer. Stretched sail.
I have counted half the catalogue of ships:
That caravan of cranes, that expansive shoal
Which once shrouded Hellas.

Like a wedge of cranes towards strange countries
(On the heads of kings the spray of gods),
Where are you sailing? Without Helen
What could Troy mean to you, Achaean men?

All is moved by love: Homer, the sea.
To which shall I listen? Homer speaks silently.
And the black sea, thunderous orator,
Breaks on my pillow with a roar.

(78)   1915

Herds of horses graze or gaily neigh,
The valley rusts like Rome;
Time's translucent rapids wash away
A classical Spring's dry gold.

This year in the Autumn while
I trample oak-leaves on deserted paths
I remember Caesar's lovely profile:
Effeminate features, treacherous hook-nose.

Forum and Capitol far away, nature is drooping:
Even here, on the world's rim, I hear
The era of Augustus rolling,
Majestic as an orb.

When I am old may my sadness gleam.
I was born in Rome; it has come back to me;
My she-wolf was kind Autumn;
August – month of the Caesars – smiled on me.

(80)   1915

First published by Struve/Filippov, 1964

You have fallen for the hunters' lure:
Stag, the forests shall mourn!

Make off with my black coat, o sun;
But keep safe my staying-power!

(165)   1913

In Euripides the old men,
An abject throng, shamble out
Like sheep. I follow the snake's path,
In my heart – dark injury.

But it'll not be long
Before I shake off sadness,
Like a boy in the evening
Shaking sand from his sandals.

(178)   1914

From *TRISTIA* *(1922)*

– How the splendour of these veils and of this dress
Weighs me down in my disgrace!

    – In stony Troezen there shall be
    A notorious disaster,
    The royal stairs
    Shall redden with shame
    . . .
    . . .
    And a black sun rise
    For the amorous mother.

– Oh if it were hatred seething in my breast, –
But, you see, the confession burst from my own lips.

    – In the white of noon Phaedra burns
    With a black flame.
    In the white of noon
    A funeral taper smoulders.
    Hippolytus, beware of your mother:
    Phaedra – the night – makes eyes at you
    In the white of noon.

– With my black love I've sullied the sun . . .
. . .

    – We're afraid, we don't dare
    To succour the imperial grief.
    Stung by Theseus, night fell on him.
    We'll bring the dead home with our burial chant;
    We'll cool the black sun
    Of its savage, insomniac passion.

(82)   1916

We shall leave our bones in transparent Petropolis,
Where Proserpina rules over us.
We drink the deadly air with every breath,
And every hour is the anniversary of our death.
Goddess of the sea, thunderous Athena,
Remove your mighty helmet of stone.
In transparent Petropolis we shall leave only bone:
Here Proserpina is tsar.

(89)   1916

This night is irredeemable.
Where you are, it is still light.
At Jerusalem's gates
A black sun has risen.

The yellow sun is more tormenting –
Hush-a-bye, baby.
Jews in the bright temple
Buried my mother.

Bereft of priests, devoid of grace,
Jews in the bright temple
Sang the service
Over her ashes.

The voice of Israelites rang out
Over this woman.
I woke in a radiant cradle,
Lit by a black sun.

(91)   1916

Disbelieving the miracle of resurrection,
We wandered through the cemetery.
– The earth, you know, everywhere
Reminds me of those hills

. . .

. . .

Where Russia stops abruptly
Above the black and deafly-roaring sea.

An ample field runs down
From these monastic slopes.
I didn't want to travel south,
Away from the spaciousness of Vladimir,
But to stay with that lacklustre nun
In this dark wooden village of god's fools
Would have spelled disaster.

I kiss your sunburnt elbow
And a wax-like patch of forehead –
Still white, I know,
Under a strand of dark-complexioned gold.
I kiss your hand whose turquoise bracelet
Leaves a strip of white:
Here in Tauris the ardent summers
Work such wonders.

How quickly you went dark
And came to the Redeemer's meagre icon
And couldn't be torn away from kissing –
You who in Moscow had been the proud one.
For us only a name remains –
A sound miraculous and lasting.
Take from me these grains of sand:
I'm pouring them from hand to hand.

(90)   1916

Out of the bottle the stream of golden honey poured so slowly
That she had time to murmur (she who'd invited us):
Here, in sad Tauris, where fate has led us,
We shan't be bored. – She glanced over her shoulder.

Everywhere the rites of Bacchus, as if the world
Were only watchmen, dogs; you'll not meet anyone:
Like heavy barrels the peaceful days roll on;
Far-off voices in a hut – you neither understand them nor reply.

After tea we came into the great brown garden,
Dark blinds lowered like eyelids on the windows,
Past white columns to see the grapes
Where sun-lit glass has sluiced the sleepy mountain.

The vine, I said, lives on like ancient battles –
Leafy-headed horsemen fight in flowery flourishes.
Knowledge of Hellas is here in stony Tauris –
And the golden acres, rusty furrows.

Well, in the white room silence stays like a spinning-wheel.
A smell of vinegar and paint, and wine fresh from the cellar.
Do you remember, in the Grecian house, the wife dear to all:
Not Helen – the other – how long she spent spinning?

Golden fleece, where are you, golden fleece?
The whole journey a thundering of the sea's weighty waves.
And leaving his ship, canvas worn-out on the seas,
Odysseus came back, filled with time and space.

(92)   1917

Spring's clear grey
Asphodel
Is far away.
Sand rustles, waves seethe.
Like Persephone my soul shall enter
The light-hearted circle:
In the kingdom of the dead you cannot unbury
Arms sunburnt as these.

Why do we entrust to a boat
The weight of a funeral urn,
And celebrate the black rose festival
On amethyst-coloured water?
My soul aspires there,
Unto the misty promontory of Meganom,
And a black sail shall come back from there
After the burial!

A shadowy column of storm-clouds
Quickly passes,
Under a windy moon
Black rose-flakes scurry.
And memory's huge flag –
Bird of death and mourners –
Trails its black edges
Over the cypress poop.

And the sad fan of years gone by
Opens with a rustling sigh
Where the amulet was darkly buried
With a shudder in the sand.
My soul aspires there,
Unto the misty promontory of Meganom,
And a black sail shall come back from there
After the burial!

(93)　1917

Tristia

I've studied the science of goodbyes
From bareheaded laments at night.
Oxen chew, waiting lengthens,
This last hour of vigil in the city.
And I honour the rituals of its cock-crowing night
When, having lifted the journey's burden of grief,
Tear-stained eyes gaze into the distance
And singing of Muses blends with the weeping of women.

Who can know from the word *goodbye*
What kind of separation lies before us,
What the cock's clamour promises
When a light burns in the acropolis,
And at the dawn of some sort of new life
When the lazy ox chews in his stall
Why the rooster, herald of new life,
Flaps his wings on the city walls?

And I like the way of weaving:
The shuttle runs, the spindle hums,
And – flying to meet us like swan's down –
Look, barefooted Delia!
Oh how meagre life's weft,
How threadbare the language of happiness!
Everything existed of old, everything happens again,
And only the moment of recognition is sweet.

So be it: on a clean clay dish
Lies a translucent shape
Like a squirrel's pelt,
And a girl, transfixed, stares at the wax.
Not for us to guess at Grecian Erebus;
Wax is for women what bronze is for men.
On us our fate falls only in battles;
Their death is given in divination.

(104)   1918

Sisters: heaviness and sweetness – the same insignia.
Wasps and bees suck the heavy rose.
Man dies, the hot sand cools.
Yesterday's sun lies on a black litter.

Oh, heavy honeycombs, sweetness of nets:
It's easier to raise a rock than to know your essence!
I'm left with one aim only, a golden one:
To free myself from the burden of time.

I drink the turbid air as if it were dark water.
Time is turned by the plough, and the rose was earth.
The heavy-sweet roses, in their slow whirlpool,
Are plaited into double wreaths.

(108)   1920

Return to the incestuous lap,
Leah, from which you came:
Instead of Ilium's sun
You chose a yellow twilight.

Go, no one shall touch you.
On the father's breast, at dead of night,
Let an incestuous daughter
Bury her head.

But a fateful change
Must be fulfilled in you:
You shall be called Leah – not Helen – ,
Not because imperial blood

Flows heavier in those veins
Than yours.
No, you shall fall in love with a Jew
And dissolve in him. The Lord be with you.

(109)   1920

When Psyche, who is life, descends among shades,
Pursuing Persephone through half-transparent leaves,
The blind swallow hurls itself at her feet,
With Stygian affection and a green twig.

Phantoms in a throng speed towards their new companion,
They meet the fugitive with grievings,
In her face they wring weak hands,
Perplexed by diffident expectations.

One holds out a mirror, another a phial of perfumes –
The soul likes trinkets, is after all feminine.
And dry complainings, like fine rain,
Sprinkle the leafless forest with transparent voices.

And not knowing what to do in this friendly hubbub,
The soul doesn't recognise the transparent trees.
She breathes on the mirror, slow to hand over
The lozenge of copper to the master of the ferry.

(112)   1920

I have forgotten the word I wanted to say.
On severed wings, to play with the transparent ones,
The blind swallow flies back to her palace of shadows.
Night songs are sung in frenzied absentmindedness.

No birds are heard. No blossom on the immortelle.
The manes of the night horses are transparent.
An empty boat floats on an arid estuary
And, lost among grasshoppers, the word swoons.

It slowly grows, like a tent or shrine,
Now throws itself down like demented Antigone,
Now like a dead swallow falls at one's feet,
With Stygian affection and a green twig.

Oh to bring back the shyness of clairvoyant fingers,
Recognition's rounded happiness!
I am so afraid of the sobbing of the Muses,
Of mist, of bells, of brokenness.

They who are going to die can love and see,
Even sound can pour into their fingers,
But I have forgotten what I wanted to say
And a thought without flesh flies back to its palace of shadows.

The transparent one keeps on saying the wrong thing:
Always *swallow, my love, Antigone* . . .
And on my lips the black ice burns,
The recollection of Stygian clamour.

(113)   1920

For the sake of delight
Take from my hands some sun and some honey,
As Persephone's bees enjoined on us.

Not to be untied, the unmoored boat;
Not to be heard, fur-shod shadows;
Not to be silenced, life's thick terrors.

Now we have only kisses,
Bristly and crisp like bees,
Which die when they fly from the hive.

Their home is the dense forest of Taigetos,
They rustle in transparent thickets of night,
Fed by time, by honeysuckle and mint.

For the sake of delight then, take my uncouth present:
This simple necklace of dead dried bees
That turned honey into sun.

(116)   1920

Here is the pyx, it hangs in the air
Like a golden sun – a splendid moment,
Now only the Greek tongue should be heard:
Taking the whole world in one's hands like an apple.

It is the solemn zenith of the service,
Light in the circular temple in July under the dome,
So that wholeheartedly we sigh, beyond time,
Over that meadow where time stands still.

And the Eucharist hovers like an eternal midday –
All participate, play and sing;
And in the sight of all the holy vessel pours
In a never-ending gladdening.

(117)   1920

Because I had to let go of your arms,
Because I betrayed your salty tender lips,
I must wait for dawn in the dense acropolis.
How I abhor these weeping ancient timbers!

Achaean men fit out the Horse in the dark,
Cut vigorously into walls with toothed saws,
Nothing can quiet the blood's dry murmur,
And you have no name, no sound, no copy.

How could I think you'd come back, how could I dare?
Why did I run away from you before it was time?
The gloom hasn't lightened and the cock hasn't crowed,
The hot axe hasn't yet split the wood.

The walls ooze resin like a transparent tear,
The town feels its wooden ribs,
But blood has rushed to the ladders and taken it by storm,
And the men have seen an alluring image three times in dreams.

Where is dear Troy? Where the imperial, where the maidenly
        house?
Priam's lofty starling-coop shall be a ruin.
And arrows fall like un-wet wooden rain;
And other arrows, like a nut-grove, rise from the earth.

The last star-pricks are dying out painlessly,
As morning, a grey swallow, raps at the window.
And lethargic day, like an ox woken in straw,
Stirs on the streets, tousled by long sleep.

(119)   1920

When the city moon looks out on the avenues,
And slowly lights the impenetrable town,
And darkness swells, full of melancholy and bronze,
And wax songs are smashed by the harshness of time;

And the cuckoo is weeping in its stone tower,
And the ashen woman, descending to reap the lifeless world,
Quietly scatters huge spokes of shadow
And strews yellowing straw across the floorboards . . .

(121)   1920

On my lips a singing name, I stepped
Into the ring of dancing shadows
Trampling on the tender meadow.
Everything melted except a mist of faint sound.

To begin with I thought the name was 'seraph'
And I fought shy of such a light body,
A few days passed and I blended with it,
Dissolved into favourite shadow.

And again from the apple-tree wild fruit falls,
And the secret form flickers in front of me,
And blasphemes, and curses itself,
And swallows the burning coals of jealousy.

Then happiness rolls by like a golden hoop
Fulfilling someone else's will,
And cutting the air with the palm of your hand
You chase the sweetness of Spring.

And it is so arranged that we do not dance away
From these spell-bound circles.
In virginal earth resilient hills
Lie swaddled away.

(123)   1920

I like the grey silences under the arches:
Public prayer, funeral processions,
The affecting obligatory rites and requiems at Saint Isaac's.

I like the priest's unhurried step;
The winding-sheet's expansive bodying-forth;
Lent's Galilean gloom, like an ancient fishing-net;

And smoke of the Old Testament on glowing altars,
And the priest's orphaned cry. And royal meekness –
Under impassioned purple vestments, unsullied snow.

Hagia Sophia and Saint Peter's – eternal barns of air and light,
Storehouses of everlasting goods,
Granaries of the New Testament.

Not to you is the spirit drawn in years of heaviness;
Here, along Saint Isaac's wide and sullen steps,
The wolves of tribulation slink; we shall never betray their tracks:

For the slave is free, having overcome fear,
And in cool granaries, in deep bins,
The grain of whole and perfect faith is stored.

(124)   1921

From POEMS (1928)

I was washing at night in the courtyard –
The sky's harsh stars shone out.
Starlight, like salt on an axe-head –
The rain-butt, brim-full, had frozen.

The gates are locked,
And the earth in all conscience is bleak.
There's scarcely anything
Purer than the truth of a clean towel.

A star melts, like salt, in the barrel
And the freezing water is blacker,
Death more lucid, misfortune saltier,
And the earth more truthful, more awful.

(126)   1921

To some, winter is a blue sky of steaming wine and nuts,
To some a fragrant punch of cinnamon,
Some get their salty orders from the brutal stars
To carry back to smoke-filled huts.

A little still-warm chicken dung,
Sheep's muddle-headed warmth:
For the care I need, for a lighted match, for life,
I'll give everything.

Look: in my hand there's only an earthenware bowl;
A twittering prophecy of stars is tickling my thin ear;
Through this pitiful plumage I have to admire
The yellowness of grass and the warmth of the soil.

Quietly to be carding wool and tedding straw;
To starve like an apple-tree in its winter binding;
Senselessly drawn by tenderness for everything alien;
Fumbling through emptiness, patiently waiting.

Let the conspirators, like sheep, speed over the snow.
Let the brittle snow-crust crack.
Winter – to some – is a lodging of wormwood and acrid smoke,
To some the stern salt of solemn injury and lack.

Oh to raise a lantern on a long stick;
My dog in front, to walk – under the salt of the stars –
Into a soothsayer's yard, bringing a cock
For the cauldron. The white, white snow scalds my eyes till they
    smart.

(127)   1922

Rosy foam of fatigue on his sensual lips,
The bull furiously paws at the green breakers;
A ladies' man, no oarsman, he snorts,
His spine unused to its laborious burden.

Now and then a dolphin leaps in an arc
Or a creature with prickles swims by.
Hold his worldly goods in your arms, gentle Europa:
Where could a bull find a more desirable yoke?

Bitterly she heeds the mighty splashing:
The corpulent and fertile sea is seething.
Aghast at the water's oily brilliance,
She'd like to climb down those hirsute cliffs.

Ah, she'd prefer the company of sheep,
The creak of rowlocks or the lap of a spacious deck,
And fish flashing past a loftier poop. –
But the oarless oarsman swims with her further and further!

(128)   1922

As the leaven swells,
So the housewife's well-disposed soul
Is possessed by the heat of the loaves,

As if Sophias of bread
Raise cupolas of rounded ardour
From a table of cherubim

And to coax a miraculous surplus
With force or caresses
The kingly herd-boy, time, seizes the loaf, the word.

Even the stale step-son of the centuries
Finds his place – as the drying makeweight
Of loaves already taken from the oven.

(130)   1922

I climbed into the tousled hayloft,
Breathed the hay-dust of the mouldering stars,
The dishevelment of space,

And on the ladder pondered: why
Wake up a swarm of sounds, the miracle of Aeolian order,
Athwart this everlasting squabble?

Once more I want to rustle
Something out of nothing –
To blaze like a match, shoulder the night, wake it up.

The huge and shaggy load sticks out above the universe,
The hayloft's ancient chaos
Begins to tickle as the darkness swells.

Mowers bring back
Goldfinches fallen from their nests.
I shall wring loose from these burning lines,

Get back to the order of sound where I belong,
To the blood's grass-like and ringing connection,
Nerving myself for the dream beyond reason.

(*from* 131 *and* 132)   1922

My time

My time, my brute, who dares
To look you in the eyes
And glue together with his blood
The backbones of two centuries?
Blood the builder gushes
From the gullet of the earth,
It's only parasites that tremble
On the future's threshold.

To wrench our age out of prison
We need a flute, to connect
The joints of days now tumoured . . .

And buds shall swell again,
Shoots gush out greenly.
But your backbone is broken,
My beautiful, pitiful century.
With an idiot's harsh and feeble grin
You look behind:
A beast, once supple,
Ponders its paw-marks in the sand.

(*from* 135)   1923

We look at a forest and say:
Here is a forest for ships and masts,
Red pines,
Free to their tops of their shaggy burden,
To creak in the storm
In the furious forestless air;
The plumbline fastened to the dancing deck
Will hold out under the wind's salt heel
And the sea-wanderer,
In his unbridled thirst for space,
Dragging through damp ruts a geometer's needle,
Collates the rough surface of the seas
With the attraction of the earth's lap.

But breathing the smell
Of resinous tears oozing through planks,
Admiring the boards of bulkheads riveted
Not by the peaceful Bethlehem carpenter but by that other,
Father of journeys, friend of seafarers,
We say:
These too stood on the earth,
Awkward as a donkey's backbone,
Their crests forgetful of their roots,
On a celebrated mountain ridge;
And howled under the sweet cloud-burst,
Fruitlessly offering the sky their precious freight
For a pinch of salt.

Where shall we begin?
Everything pitches and cracks,
The air quivering with comparisons,
No word better than another,
The earth buzzing with metaphors.
And light two-wheeled chariots,
Harnessed brightly to flocks of strenuous birds,
Explode,
Vying with the snorting favourites of the race-track.

Blest three times over whoever puts a name into song;
A song adorned with a name
Lives longer among the others,
Marked by a head-band
That frees it from forgetfulness and stupefying smells,
Whether proximity of man, fur of beast,
Or a whiff of thyme rubbed in the palms.

The air dark like water, everything alive swims in it like fish
Undulating through the sphere –
Compact, resilient, hardly-heated –,
That crystal in which wheels move, horses shy,
The humid black-earth every night thrown up anew
By pitchforks, tridents, hoes and ploughs.
The air is mixed as densely as the earth –
You can't get out, to get inside is arduous.

Rustling runs through the trees like a green ball-game;
Children play knucklebones with the vertebrae of dead animals.
The fragile calculation of the years of our era ends.
Let's be grateful for what we had:
I too made mistakes, lost my way, lost count.
The era rang like a golden sphere,
Cast, hollow, supported by no one.
Touched, it answered *yes* and *no*,
As a child will say:
I'll give you an apple, or: *I won't give you one;*
Its face an exact copy of the voice that pronounces these words.

The sound is still ringing although its source has ceased.
The horse foams in the dust.
But the acute curve of his neck
Preserves the memory of the race with outstretched legs
When there were not four
But as many as the stones on the road,
Renewed in four shifts
As blazing hooves pushed off from the ground.

So,
Whoever finds a horseshoe
Blows away the dust,
Rubs it with wool till it shines,

Then
Hangs it over the threshold
To rest,
No longer to strike sparks from flint.
Human lips
          which have nothing more to say
Preserve the form of the last word said.
And the arm retains the sense of weight
Though the jug
          splashed half-empty
                    on the way home.

What I am saying at this moment is not being said by me
But is dug from the ground like grains of petrified wheat.
Some
      on their coins depict a lion,
Others
      a head;
Various tablets of brass, of gold and bronze
Lie with equal honour in the earth.
The century, trying to bite through them, left its teeth-marks
    there.
Time pares me down like a coin,
And there's no longer enough of me for myself.

(136) 1923

1 January 1924

Whoever's been kissing time's tortured crown
Later with filial tenderness shall recall
How time lay down to sleep
In the wheaten snow-drift beyond the window.
Whoever lifted the sick eyelids of the age –
Two vast and sleepy eye-balls –
Hears everlastingly the roaring of the rivers
Of false and desolate times.

The potentate-era has orbs like sleepy apples
And a lovely clay mouth.
But it shall fall, dying
On the overwhelmed arm of its aging son.
I know life's exhalations weaken day by day.
A little more, and the simple songs of palpable injuries
Will have been cut short,
Lips sealed with tin.

Earthenware existence! Dying era!
What I dread is this: that you'll be understood
Only by someone whose smile is helpless,
By someone who's lost.
What anguish – to search for a lost word,
To lift sick eyelids,
And with lime-corroded blood
Gather night grasses for an alien tribe.

What an era: layers of lime in the sick son's blood
Harden. Moscow sleeps, like a wooden box,
And there's nowhere to run to from the tyrant-epoch . . .
Snow, as of old, smells of apples.
I want to escape from my own doorway.
Where to? The street is dark
And conscience shows up ahead of me, white,
Like salt scattered on a pavement.

    . . .

How could I ever betray to shameful scandal –
Again the frost smells of apples –
That marvellous oath to the Fourth Estate
And vows solemn enough for tears?

Who else shall you kill? Who else extol?
What lie shall you invent?
The Underwood's cartilage – quick, wrench its key out
And you'll find the little bone of a pike;
And the layers of lime in the sick son's blood shall thaw
And blissful laughter splash out . . .
But the typewriters' simple sonatina
Is merely a shadow of the mighty sonatas.

(*from* 140)   1924

Two poems published in Novyy Mir, 1931 and 1932

Armenia

(3)
Armenia, you call for colours –
And with his paw a lion
Seizes half-a-dozen crayons from a pencil-box.

Here the women pass,
Stark as children's drawings.
They bestow their splendour,
Their lionesque beauty,
And do not terrorise the blood.

(4)
I've fingered my dishevelled life, like a mullah his Koran;
I've frozen time and haven't spilt hot blood . . .

(7)
Majesty of clamorous boulders –
Armenia! Armenia!
Summoning raucous hills to war –
Armenia! Armenia!

Unendingly journeying towards the silver trumpets of Asia –
Armenia! Armenia!
Lavishly scattering the Persian coins of the sun –
Armenia! Armenia!

(13)

Earthenware, azure . . . azure, clay . . .
What more is needed? Squint quickly,
Like a myopic shah, over a turquoise ring,
Over earth's mould, whose script and lexicon are ringing,
A festering text, a costly clay,
By which we are tormented, stirred,
As by music and the word.

(*from* parts 3, 4, 7 *and* 13 *of* 203-215)   1930

Batyushkov

Palaver of the waves . . .
Harmony of tears . . .
The bell of brotherhood . . .

Mumbling, you bring us
The grape flesh, poetry,
To refresh the palate.

Pour your eternal dreams, samples of blood,
From one glass to another.

(*from* 261)   1932

Poems published posthumously

Self-portrait

In the raised head, a hint of wing –
But the coat is flapping;
In the closed eyes, in the peace
Of the arms: instinct's pure hiding-place.

Here is a creature that can fly and sing,
The word malleable and flaming,
And congenital awkwardness is overcome
By inborn rhythm!

(164)   1931

I was only in a childish way connected with the world of power:
I was terrified of oysters and glanced distrustfully at guardsmen;
And not a grain of my soul owes it anything,
However hard I tried to look like someone else.

I never stood under the Egyptian portico of a bank
With ponderous importance, frowning, in a beaver-fur mitre,
And above the lemon-coloured Neva
No gypsy girl ever danced for me to the crackle of hundred-rouble
    notes.

Sensing future executions, from the howl of stormy events
I ran to the Black Sea nymphs,
And from the beauties of that time – from those tender European
    ladies –
How much I was granted of confusion, strain and grief!

Why does this city still retain
Its ancient rights over my thoughts and feelings?
Fire and frost have made it more insolent:
Narcissistic, doomed, frivolous, youthful!

Perhaps because in a picture-book I saw
Lady Godiva and her dissolute ginger mane,
I now repeat to myself on the sly:
Goodbye, Lady Godiva . . . Godiva, goodbye . . .

(222)   Leningrad, 1931

Wolf

For the resounding glory of eras to come,
For the lofty tribe of people then,
I've relinquished the cup at the elders' feast
And my happiness and honour.

Our times' wolf-hound grips my back,
Although I am no wolf by blood;
Squeeze me, rather, like a hat up the sleeve
Of that rough warm coat, the steppe, –

In case I see any trembling or offal
Or blood-splashed bones on the rack,
So blue polar foxes may shine for me
All night in their original beauty.

Lead me into the night where the Yenisey flows
And the pine-trees reach the stars;
Because I am no wolf by blood,
Me – only an equal shall murder.

(227)   1931

I drink to the blossoming epaulette,
To all I'm reproached for and won't forget:

Asthma and lordly fur-coat,
Bile of the Petersburg climate,

Singing pines of Savoy,
Jug of cream and Alpine joy,

Oil paintings from Paris. And I rejoice
At roses in the Rolls-Royce,

The Champs-Elysées benzine,
Proud English red-heads, quinine.

To the waves of Biscay! I drink, but what with I'm not sure:
The Pope's Châteauneuf, a happy Spumante, or . . .?

(233)   1931

Help me, O Lord, to survive this night:
I fear for life – your slave. –
Living in Petersburg is like sleeping in a grave.

(223)   1931

Impressionism

The painter has portrayed for us
Lilac's deep swoon,
And colour's sonorous gradations
Cover his canvas with scabs.

He knew the density of oil,
Its pastry summer
Baked with violet marrow
Distended swelteringly.

Even more violet is that shadow there:
A violin-bow or whip, dying like a match,
So that you'd say: chefs in the kitchen
Are sizzling plump pigeons.

Veils merely sketched,
A swing you have to guess.
And now, in this sunny disorder,
A bee keeps house.

(258)   1932

Ariosto

It's cold in Europe. Italy is dark.
And power is barbarous like the hands of the beard-shaver.
Oh to throw wide open, as soon as possible,
A vast window on the Adriatic.

And I delight in his frenzied leisure:
Babble of sweet and sour, lovely oyster-sounds –
The whirring of a hundred whips.
With my knife I shrink from laying bare the pearl.

Through his window he smiles at the butcher's stall:
The child asleep under a net of blue flies;
The soldiers of the Duke now drunk
On wine and garlic and on plague.

Dear Ariosto, maybe a century shall pass –
And we shall pour your azure and our black together
Into one fraternal, vast, blue-black sea.
We were there too. We too drank mead.

(*from* 267 *and* 268)   1933, 1936

We exist, without sensing our country beneath us.
Ten steps away our words can't be heard.

But where there are enough of us for half a conversation
They always commemorate the Kremlin mountaineer.

His fat fingers slimy as worms,
His words dependable as weights of measure.

The cockroach moustaches chuckle,
His top-boots gleam.

And round him a riff-raff of scraggy-necked chiefs;
He plays with these half men, lackeys,

Who warble, or miaow, or whimper.
He alone prods and probes.

He forges decree after decree like horseshoes:
In the groin, brain, forehead, eye.

Whoever's being executed – there's raspberry compote
And the gigantic torso of the Georgian.

(286)   1933

1. The body of King Arshak is unwashed, his beard runs wild.
2. His fingernails are broken, and wood-lice crawl across his face.
3. His ears, grown dull with silence, once listened to Greek music.
4. His tongue is scabbed from jailer's food – which once pressed grapes against the sky and was adroit like the tip of a flautist's tongue.
5. The seed of Arshak has withered in his scrotum and his voice is sparse as the bleating of a sheep.
6. King Shapukh, thinks Arshak, has got the better of me and, worse, has taken my air for himself!
7. The Assyrian holds my heart in his hand.
8. He commands my hair and fingernails. He grows my beard and swallows my spit, so used has he become to the thought that I am to be found here – in the fortress of Aniush.
9. The Kushan people rose up against Shapukh.
10. They snapped the border like silken thread.
11. Like an eyelash in his eye, the attack pricked King Shapukh.
12. Both enemies screwed up their eyes, so as not to see each other.
13. Darmastat, the most gracious and best-educated of the eunuchs, encouraged the commander of the cavalry, at the centre of Shapukh's army. He wormed his way into favour, snatched his master, like a chess-piece, out of danger, remaining all the while in public view.
14. He had been governor of the province of Andekh in the days when Arshak's velvet voice gave orders.
15. Yesterday Arshak was a king, but today is fallen into a crevice, huddles like a baby in the womb, and warms himself with lice, enjoying the itch.
16. When the time came for his reward, Darmastat's request tickled the Assyrian's keen ears like a feather:
17. Give me a pass to the fortress of Aniush. I should like Arshak to spend one more day, full of sounds, taste and smell, as it used to be when he entertained himself at the chase and saw to the planting of trees.

(from *Journey to Armenia*; from 8. 'Alagez')   1933

Your narrow shoulders are to redden under scourges,
Redden under scourges and to burn in frosts.

Your child-like arms are to lift heavy irons,
To lift heavy irons and to sew mail-bags.

Your tender soles are to walk barefoot on glass,
Barefoot on glass and blood-stained sand.

And I am here to burn for you like a black candle,
Burn like a black candle and not dare to pray.

(296)   1934

Black earth

Much-esteemed, too black, all in peak-condition,
This earth is groomed fetlocks, air and care;
Crumbling, coming together, like a choir –
Wet clods of my 'soil and freedom'!

In the days of early ploughing – black, almost blue;
And this is the ground of weaponless work.
A thousand mounds of furrowed language:
And something unbounded within these bounds.

And yet the earth is – a blunder, a blunt axe-head.
One can implore it, fall at its feet:
Still it whets the hearing like a mildewed flute,
It ploughs the ear with a chilly, morning clarinet.

How pleasing fatty topsoil is to ploughshare,
How silent the steppe in its April upheaval!
Well, I wish you well, black earth: be firm, sharp-eyed . . .
In labour is a black-voiced silence.

(299)   April 1935

Yes, I'm lying in the earth, moving my lips,
But what I'm going to say every schoolboy shall know by heart:

The earth is at its roundest on Red Square
And its unenslaved curve is hard,

On Red Square the earth is at its roundest
And its curve, rolling all the way down to the rice-fields,

Is unexpectedly exuberant,
So long as a last slave is living on this earth.

(306)   May 1935

You took away my seas, and running jumps, and sky.
The violent earth propped my foot.
Where could this clever move get you?
You couldn't take away my mumbling lips.

(307)   May 1935

My country conversed with me,
Spoiled, scolded, didn't read me.
But when I grew up as an eye-witness,
Then she took note. Like a lens
With a beam from the Admiralty dockyard
She set me on fire.

(*part 6 of* 312)   May – June 1935

Those hundred-carat ingots, Roman nights,
Those breasts that for young Goethe were a lure:

Let me be answerable, but not lose all my rights.
Life still exists outside the law.

(316)   June 1935

82

The wave advances – one wave breaking another's backbone,
Flinging itself at the moon in slavish yearning.
And these young janissaries –
The tireless metropolis of breakers –
Rave, slant-eyed, and dig their ditch in sand.

But through the flaky gloom
An unbuilt wall's pale teeth rise up.
From foaming stairs the soldiers of suspicious sultans
Crash – smashed into spray.
Cold eunuchs bring the poison in.

(319)   July 1935

I shall perform a smoky rite:
In this opal here, in my disgrace,
I see a seaside summer's strawberries –
Cleft cornelians
And their brothers, ant-like agates.

But a pebble from the sea's depths,
A simple soldier,
Is more dear to me:
Grey, wild,
That no one wants.

(318)   July 1935

I shall not return my borrowed dust to the earth,
Like a white, floury butterfly.
I desire this thinking body
To turn into a street, a country –
This vertebral, charred flesh,
Conscious of its span.

(*from* 320)   21 July 1935

Now today is yellow-mouthed, idiotic:
I can't make sense of it.
Dock gates stare at me
Through anchors and mist.

Over faded water a convoy of battleships
Moves quietly, quietly,
Looking, under the ice of the canals,
Blacker than lead pencils in narrow pencil-boxes.

(329)   9 – 28 December 1936

Like a belated present,
Winter is now palpable:
I like its initial,
Diffident sweep.

Its terror is beautiful,
Like the beginning of dreadful deeds:
Even ravens are alarmed
By the leafless circle.

But more powerful than anything
Is its infirmly-bulging blueness:
The half-formed ice on the river's brow,
Lullabying unsleepingly . . .

(336)   29 – 30 December 1936

I would sing of him who shifted the axis of the world . . .
See, Aeschylus, how I weep as I draw the portrait of
     the Leader . . .
In the friendship of his wise eyes
One suddenly sees – a father! . . .
(His *powerful* eyes – sternly kind . . .)
And I want to thank the hills
That nourished this gristle, this wrist.
He was born in the mountains and knew the bitterness
     of prison.

I want to call him – not Stalin – but Dzhugashvili!
I seem to see him dressed in his greatcoat and his cap,
On the wonderful square, with his *happy* eyes . . .
The furrows of his giant plough reach the sun.
He smiles with the smile of the harvester . . .

(*from* 'Lines on Stalin')   1937

I still haven't died, I'm still not alone,
While – with a beggar-woman for companion –
I'm delighted by the immense plains,
And the haze, and hunger, and snow-storms.

I live in miraculous poverty, opulent privation –
Alone, at peace, consoled;
These days and nights are hallowed,
And honey-voiced this innocent labour.

Unhappy any man whom, like his shadow,
A dog's bark scares and the wind scythes down.
And poor indeed one who, half-alive,
Begs favour of a shadow.

(354)   15 – 16 January 1937

I look the frost in the face, alone –
It's going nowhere, I come from nowhere,
And still the breathing plain is ironed
Miraculously, folded without a crease.

The sun is squinting in laundered destitution,
Its frown peaceful and consoled,
The multitude of forests much the same . . .
Snow crunches in my eyes, innocent as bread.

(349)   16 January 1937

Asthmatic sloth of asphyxiating steppes!
Sick to death of space,
The horizon breathes – it pulsates and swells –
And a blindfold is what I need!

I'd prefer to have borne the disposition
Of leaf-like layers of sand on the Kama's toothy shores.
I'd have clung to its shy sleeves,
Its ripples, brinks and holes.

We'd have worked in harmony – for a century or a second.
Envious of the rapids' precipitation,
I'd have listened under drifting bark
To the fibrous procession of the rings.

(351)   16 January 1937

Plagued by miraculous hunger,
What can we do with the murderous plains?
Isn't it that what we deem their openness
We falling asleep behold, eyes open –
And everywhere the questions swell – where do they go,
And where do they come from?
And is not he who makes us, sleeping, shriek,
Slowly crawling across them –
The Judas of all future men?

(350)   16 January 1937

Don't compare: anything alive is matchless.
I yield, with tender terror,
To the plainness of the plains – that level everything.
The sky's sphere has made me ill.

I appealed to the air, my servant,
Waiting for service or news;
I prepared for a journey, swam along the arc
Of voyages which would never start.

I'm ready to wander where I shall have more sky.
But that bright longing cannot release me now
From the still-young hills of Voronezh
To the bright, all-human ones of Tuscany.

(352)   18 January 1937

What has contended with oxide and alloys
Burns like feminine silver,
And quiet work silvers the iron
Of the plough, the voice of the poet.

(353)   1937

The mounds of human heads disappear into the distance,
I dwindle there, no longer noticed,
But in affectionate books, in children's games,
I shall rise from the dead to say: the sun!

(341)   1937

I'm listening, listening to the early ice
Rustling under bridges,
It brings to mind bright drunkenness
Drifting above our heads.

From stale stairways, from areas
Of awkward palaces
On the edges of his Florence,
Alighieri sang more forcefully
From tired lips.

So too my shadow picks
At the grain of the granite,
Eyeing in the dark a row of hulks
That seemed houses in the light,

Or twiddles its thumbs, is lazy,
Yawns with us,
Is noisy,
Warmed by other people's wine and sky,

And feeds stale loaves
To the importunate swans . . .

(358)   22 January 1937

A little boy, his red face shining like a lamp,
Lord and master of his sledge,
Careers across the steaming ice

And I – at odds with the obedient world – rejoice
In the contagion of toboggans,
Amazed by children racing over water:

Steep slopes, silver runners, frosty exhalations.
Oh that our era might slide for ever,
Soundless as squirrels, towards a soft river . . .

(359)   24 January 1937

Where can I put myself this January?
The city, exposed, is extravagantly stubborn . . .
Am I drunk on doors that lock me out?
The catches and fastenings make me want to roar.

And yapping alleys stretched like stockings,
Streets tangled as an attic,
And cornered creatures crawling into corners
And scuttling out on the sly.

And I slither into a pit, into the calloused dark,
Towards the iced-up pump-house,
And, stumbling, munch dead air,
And the feverish rooks rise up.

And I gasp after them, hammering
On some frozen wood-pile:
Just a reader, someone to speak with, a doctor!
A conversation on the twisted stairs!

(360)   February 1937

Like Rembrandt, martyr of light and dark,
I've gone into the depths of time –
And found it numb.
One rib of mine's a burning spike
Which is not guarded by these watchmen,
Nor by this sentry, asleep under the storm.

Forgive me, magnificent brother, and master,
And father of the black-green darkness . . .
Like a little boy, following grown-ups into wrinkled water,
I seem to be walking towards a future,
But it seems I'll never see it,
Now that our tribe is troubled by a shadow,
Twilight's intoxications, years for ever hollow.

(*from* 265 *and* 364)   Summer 1931 and 4 February 1937

Breaks of the rounded bays, shingle like cartilage, the blue,
And the slow sail continued as a cloud –
I'm parted from you, scarcely having known your worth.
Longer than organ fugues and bitter is the false-haired seaweed,
Smelling of long-contracted falsities.
My head is tipsy with an iron tenderness,
Rust gnaws gently at the sloping shore . . .
Why does another sand lie under my head?
You – guttural Urals, muscular Volga,
These steppes – here are all my rights, –
And I must go on breathing in your air
With all my might.

(366)   4 February 1937

Song comes when the throat is raw and the mind is dry,
One's sight moderately moist and consciousness unwily:
Are the grapes in good condition? The wine-skins?
And the stirrings of Colchis in the blood?
But my chest tightens, I'm tongue-tied:
It's no longer me singing – my breathing sings –,
My ears sheathed in mountains, my head empty.

An unmercenary song is its own reward:
Delight for dear ones, tar for adversaries.

Single-eyed songs grow out of moss,
Single-voiced offerings chanted on horses, on hills:
In quivering veins their blood is astir –
These hunters imbibe the wine, inhale the air.
A vexed and generous justice is their care:
They single-mindedly betroth and bring
The young pair, sinless, to their wedding.

(365)   8 February 1937

Eyes keener than a sharpened scythe –
In the pupil a cuckoo, a drop of dew, –

Now barely able – stretched full-length –
To pick out a single group of stars.

(368)   8 – 9 February 1937

Equipped with the eyesight and absorption of wasps
That sip and suck at the earth's axis,
I sense everything it's my fate to witness
And fruitlessly possess its core.

I neither sing, nor draw,
Nor scrape a black-voiced bow across a string:
I only sting into life, and love
To envy the energy of subtle wasps.

Oh if some day – sidestepping sleep and death –
A goad of air or summer's sting
Could pierce me into hearing
The buzz of earth, buzz of the earth.

(367)   8 February 1937

I'm plunged into a lion's den, a fort,
And sinking lower, lower, lower,
Under the yeast shower of these sounds:
Stronger than lions, more potent than the Pentateuch.

How near your summons:
Keener than commandments of childbirth, firstlings –,
Like strings of pearls at the bottom of the sea
Or baskets meekly borne by Tahitian women.

Motherland of chastening songs, come close,
The declivities deepening in your voice! – O primal mother,
The shy-sweet faces of our daughters
Aren't worth your little finger.

My time is still unbounded.
And I have accompanied the rapture of the universe
As muted organ pipes
Accompany a woman's voice.

(370)   12 February 1937

If our enemies take me
And people stop talking to me,
If they confiscate the whole world –
The right to breathe, open doors,
Affirm that existence shall go on
And that the people, like a judge, shall judge,
And if they dare to keep me like an animal
And fling my food on the floor, –
I won't fall silent or deaden the agony,
But shall write what I'm free to write,
My naked body gathering momentum like a bell,
And in a corner of the ominous dark
I'll yoke ten oxen to my voice
And move my hand in the darkness like a plough
And, wrung out into a sea of fraternal eyes,
Shall fall with the full heaviness of a harvest,
Exploding in the distance with all the precision of an oath,
And in the depths of the unguarded night
The eyes of the unskilled earth shall shine
And like a ripe thunderstorm Lenin shall burst out,
But on this earth (which shall escape decay)
There to murder life and reason – Stalin.

(372)   February 1937

Ribbed pillars and piers, arcades and aisles,
Come and go: the conscientious spider-ray
Spreads eternity's crystal cathedrals;
Life's reticulations loosen mindlessly.

A thin beam of light to join them together,
The columns of grateful pure lines
Shall gather intimately sometime or other
Like guests with an open countenance.

Only let it be now on earth, and not in heaven,
As in a house full of music. –
Good if we survive till then;
If only we don't scare or wound them.

Forgive me for what I'm saying;
Read it aloud to me quietly.

(*from* 380)   15 March 1937

This is what I want most of all:
With no one on my track
To soar behind the light –
That I couldn't be farther from;

And for you to shine in that circle –
There's no other happiness –,
To learn from a star
What light could mean.

And I'd like to tell you –
Mumbling, my little one –
That it's through our babbling
I deliver you to the light.

A star is only a star –
Light is only light –
Because our whisperings keep us warm
And our babble makes us strong.

(384)   27 March 1937

This azure island was exalted by its potters –
Crete the joyful. In the resounding earth
They baked their gift. Do you hear the dolphin fins
Beat underground?

It's easy to remember the sea,
Enraptured in its clay;
The cold power of a pot
Breaks into sea and seeing.

Azure island, volatile Crete,
Give me back what's mine – my labour;
From the breasts of the fruitful goddess
Fill the baked vessels.

This was, turned azure, and was sung,
Long before Ulysses,
Before food and drink
Were called 'my' and 'mine'.

Recover and shine again,
Star of ox-eyed heaven,
And fortuity, the flying fish,
And the sea saying *yes*.

(385)   March 1937

As if language weren't enough,
The *theta* and *iota* of a Greek flute could pine
And – carefree, unaccountable –
Cross ravines and ripen.

Impossible to forsake the flute,
With one's tongue not to press it
Into speech, not to mould a flute with lips,
And not, by clenching teeth, suppress it.

The flute player never knows repose –
It seems he is alone,
That sometime or other out of lilac clay
He formed a sea, his own.

With the urgency of remembering lips,
With an ambitious, resonant whisper,
He gathers the sounds to save them,
Spare, precise, eager.

Later we shall not be able to repeat him.
And when I'm filled with the seas,
Squeezing clods of clay to death in my hands,
My measure has changed to disease.

My own lips lisp,
Plague or murder at the root.
And involuntarily falling, falling,
I diminish the force of the flute.

(387)   7 April 1937

I raise this greenness to my lips,
This sticky promise of leaves,
This breach-of-promise earth:
Mother of maples, of oaks, of snowdrops.

See how I'm dazzled, exalted,
Obedient to the lowliest root.
And aren't my eyes miraculously
Blinded by the explosions of this park?

A green croak of frogs concatenates
Like balls of mercury;
Twigs are becoming branches;
The fallow air grows milky.

(388)   30 April 1937

With her irregular delightful way of walking
She's limping on the empty earth;
A halting freedom draws her on.
It seems that a clear surmise lingers in her gait –
Something to do with this spring weather,
Original mother of the sepulchral dome.
And this shall always be beginning.

There are women who are natives of the sodden earth:
Their every step a hollow sobbing,
Their calling to accompany the dead,
To be first to meet the risen.
And we should trespass to demand caresses of them,
And to part from them is beyond our strength . . .

But whatever shall be is a promise only.

(*from* 394)   4 May 1937

Notes

Further Reading

Notes

In this rag-bag of notes I've set out to refer to and convey as wide a spectrum of information and bibliography as is succinctly possible. As the act of translation is necessarily an act of literary criticism, my own judgements, knowledge and ignorance are mainly embodied in my renderings.

Numbers are those of the Struve/Filippov edition, given after each poem. O.M. – Osip Mandelshtam; N.M. – Nadezhda Mandelshtam.

Where references to authors are unspecific, see under Acknowledgements (at the end of these Notes) for title and publisher.

STONE (1913, 1916, 1923 and 1928)

Stone, the title of Mandelshtam's first book of poems, 'is obviously a prosaic symbol, yet timeless and in a way sacred – the material of which streets and cathedrals are made' (N. A. Nilsson, *Scando-Slavica* IX). 'The title . . . represents an etymologically justified anagram of the Greek word *Akme* . . .' (Omry Ronen, *Encyclopaedia Judaica*: 1973 Year Book).

(14) Peter France *(Poets of modern Russia)*: '"original speechlessness", the undifferentiated world which precedes poetry and human culture and whose image is the sea'.

V. Terras: 'O.M.'s nostalgia for primordial unity with the cosmos' (*Slavonic and East European Review* XVII No. 109, 1969).

'He felt poetry to be immanent in nature, to *be* there in the silence, a presence with which he could be "fused" . . . Poetry was not an occasion for sentiment, for "heart" . . .' (Clarence Brown, *Mandelstam*).

Robert Tracy has pointed out (in his *Osip Mandelstam's 'Stone'*) that later, in O.M.'s *The one who walks*, 'he seems to reply to *Silentium*: "Though music cannot save one from the abyss"'.

Fyodor Tyutchev (1803-73) also wrote a celebrated poem called *Silentium*. (See Charles Tomlinson's *Versions from Fyodor Tyutchev*.)

(31) The poet Batyushkov (1787–1855) spent the last thirty or so years of his life in an asylum (from 1821). See also No. 261.

(32) R. F. Holmes has suggested to me that the 'age-old traveller' may be Pushkin.

(54) 'Joseph': Osip is a Russian version of Joseph.

(60) Ovid was banished to Scythia.

(80) Ovid is speaking.

Tristia, the title of O.M.'s second book of poems, 'is a lament and an encomium for a splendid past, for Renaissance Venice, for Racine's France, for Hellas, above all for Petropolis . . . These cultures are seen as one, are fused into one . . . image of threatened civilisation . . . The theme of *Tristia* is summed up in a line of O.M.'s poem about Venice: "How can I escape this festive death?"' (Robert Chandler, from an unpublished article 'Mandelstam and Ezra Pound').

'In [O.M.'s] poems epochs and cultures that have become deeply stratified in language rise up before our consciousness. An individual word can summon them up . . .' (Boris Bukhshtab, *Russian Literature Triquarterly*, No. 1, 1971).

(82) Troezen was where Hippolytus died.

(89) Petropolis 'was Derzhavin's and Pushkin's name for Petersburg . . . A whole cultural tradition is threatened, dying'. 'It is not Athena, a goddess noted for her mercifulness and generosity, the goddess of wisdom, who reigns, but Proserpina, queen of the underworld' (S. Broyde).

(90) Dedicated to Marina Tsvetayeva. I have translated the poem in its original form, as given in Tsvetayeva's 'The history of one dedication' (*Oxford Slavonic Papers* XI, 1964).

(92) 'Tauris': the Crimea.

(93) 'the image of the "amulet buried in the sand" should be deciphered as "poetry addressed to the reader in posterity"' (K. Taranovsky).

[O.M.'s] visions of classical antiquity are not "Homeric", "Sapphic", or "Horatian", but Mandelstamian . . . It is "world culture", not ancient culture, that is the leitmotif of Mandelstam's poetry' (Victor Terras, 'Classical motifs in the poetry of Osip Mandelstam' (*Slavic and East European Journal*, 3, 1966).

Persephone (or Kore or Proserpina), Queen of the Underworld, spends two-thirds of the year with her mother Demeter (the Greek corn-goddess). 'This is the "light" part of the annual circle . . .' The black sail is 'still another topos of Greek mythology, known best from the myth of Theseus and Ariadne' (Victor Terras).

Line 20: 'Black rose-flakes' is an allusion to O.M.'s mother's death (see N.M., *Hope Abandoned*).

(104) Stanza 1: 'In the stillness of night a lover pronounces one tender name instead of another, and suddenly realises that this has happened once before: the words and the hair and the cock who has just crowed under the window crowed already in Ovid's *Tristia*. And he is overcome by a deep joy of recognition . . .' (O.M., 'The Word and Culture', in *Sobraniye sochineniy*).

Line 4: 'M's elegy . . . attains a genuine Latin ring, as Tynyanov observes, by introducing the entirely foreign word *vigilia*, which changes the chemistry of the whole stanza' (Henry Gifford, *Poetry in a divided world*).

Stanza 3: Clarence Brown refers to 'the special kind of cognition that takes place when a poet composes a poem. Mandelshtam declares that this is in fact recognition' ('Mandelstam's Notes Towards a Supreme Fiction', *Delos*, Austin, Texas, 1968, No. I).

Compare Fet's poem which begins: 'How threadbare our language!'

Line 25 onwards: see Pushkin, *Yevgeny Onegin* V: 4-10. 'The method [of divination] was to melt a candle into a shallow dish of water, where the suddenly cooled wax would assume odd shapes, like Rorschach blots or . . . like a cloud or the stretched pelt of a squirrel . . . Ovid's parting from his loved ones as he goes into exile is a paradigm of all partings' (Clarence Brown, *Mandelstam*).

'Erebus': name of 'a place of darkness between Earth and Hades'. Erebus is the son of Chaos, brother of Night, and father of Day.

Joseph Brodsky's version of this poem can be inspected in his *Less than One*, Viking, 1986, p. 128.

(108) Line 4 refers to the death of Pushkin. O.M.: 'Poetry is the plough which turns up *time*, so that the deepest layer of time – its black earth – appears on top.'

(109) Written in the Crimea during the Civil War when O.M. and N.M. were not yet permanently together. 'Our relationship must have aroused in him a keen awareness of his Jewish roots, a tribal feeling, a sense of kinship with his people – I was the only Jewess in his life. He thought of the Jews as being one family, hence the theme of incest . . . Leah was the name he had given to a daughter of Lot . . . One night, thinking about me, he had suddenly seen that I would come to him, as Lot's daughters had to their father.' (N.M., *Hope Abandoned*.)

(113) 'The word grows, bearing a green branch like the dove released from Noah's ark' (Lidija Ginzburg, 'The Poetics of Osip Mandelstam', *Twentieth-Century Russian Literary Criticism*, edited by Victor Erlich, Yale University Press, 1975).

(116) Bees were sacred to Persephone, 'her messengers to Man' (N. A. Nilsson, *Mandelstam: Five Poems*).

'The poetic word, metaphorically transformed into a kiss as a source of joy, is simultaneously a small, hairy bee which . . . has the orphic power of transmutation'; the necklace 'is a special artefact, composed of "dead bees", words which have perished in their normal usage; these "apian" words have reversed the normal process by converting honey into sunlight' (Tom Stableford, *The Literary Appreciation of Russian Writers*).

'the dense forest of Taigetos': the high mountain overlooking Sparta, the domain of Artemis and Apollo, where the bees produce 'not the sweet honey of Hymettos but a honey with . . . a darker and wilder taste' (Nilsson).

(119) Line 16: See the *Odyssey*, Book IV, lines 219-84.

(124) Stanza 4: In a poem written in 1916, Mandelstam alludes to Rome, Byzantium and Moscow – 'the three meetings of mankind and Providence

. . . Byzantium had perished and the Grace of God had passed over to Russia' (K. Taranovsky).

Stanza 6: Henry Gifford (private communication): 'The slave who has overcome his fear is free – to endure unhappiness . . .'

POEMS (1928)

'Mandelshtam's *Poems* register a disintegration so absolute that the magnificent tragedy of *Tristia* is no longer possible, for tragedy presupposes the existence of generally accepted values' (Robert Chandler).

(127) Stanza 5 – 'conspirators': the Soviet edition substitutes 'dark people'.

(128) 'Gentle Europa' is N.M.; the poem was written after their marriage.

(135) The question asked in the first stanza is answered in the second: the artist, the creator, can do these things.

O. Ronen refers to *Hamlet* as one of the subtexts:

'The time is out of joint; O cursed spite

That ever I was born to set it right!'

The original has four eight-line stanzas.

(136) 'this is an ode (Mandelshtam first subtitled it "a Pindaric fragment"), and, typically of the ode, it is concerned with itself, that is to say, with poetry. The world in which poetry must now exist is as turbulent as that of the forest and ship; everything cracks and shakes . . . The principal image of the poem, the horseshoe itself, is what is left of the stormy animal, now dead . . . This is human life frozen in its last attitudes, as though surprised in Herculaneum. The speaker himself now speaks in a resurrected voice, turned to stone, and time, the element that erupted . . . at line 55, finally flows like lava over everything, obliterating the very self of the speaker at the end.' (Clarence Brown, *Mandelstam*.)

'A "poem" is uniquely able to remain intact while all else changes, and hence to contact an unknown future recipient of an expected gift in which is preserved also a part of the poet' (S. Broyde).

(140) 'A crucial "New Year". Lenin is mortally ill . . .' (S. Monas, Notes to *Complete Poetry of Mandelstam*). O. Ronen's *An approach to Mandelstam* includes a commentary on this poem: 'Clay': Ronen refers to Job ('Thou hast made me as the clay; and wilt thou bring me into dust again').

Three and half stanzas are untranslated.

Line 16: Ronen: 'but the singing lips of the age are sealed . . .'

Line 21: Ronen: 'The theme of the forgotten or lost word of No. 113 . . . is reinterpreted here and in other poems of 1921-25 (Nos. 130, 131 and 136, etc.) in historical terms: the word becomes the heirloom, passed from one generation to another, or lost in transmission.'

Line 35 – 'Fourth Estate': Ronen: '*not* the press, but the *raznochintsy* or classless intelligentsia (to which Mandelstam felt that he belonged).'

Line 40 – 'the little bone of a pike': Ronen: 'Just as the horseshoe is, in *Whoever finds a horseshoe*, a talisman against hungry time, so the pike's bone . . . becomes . . . a talisman against . . . the hungry State.'

Line 42 – 'blissful laughter': 'the holiday laughter of the Saturnalia . . .' etc.

Line 44 – 'the mighty sonatas': Ronen points to a passage from Mandelshtam's prose work *The Noise of Time* in which Herzen is mentioned, 'whose stormy political thought will always sound like a Beethoven sonata.'

(261) The original has six four-line stanzas.

POEMS PUBLISHED POSTHUMOUSLY

(203-215) Part 7: Catullus: 'Ad claras Asiae volemus urbes'.

(164) This may be as much a portrait of Afanasy Fet as a self-portrait.

(222) Lady Godiva: 'In 1040 Leofric, Earl of Mercia and Lord of Coventry, imposed certain exactions on his tenants, which his Lady besought him to remove. He said he would do so if she would ride naked through the town.' (Brewer's *Dictionary of Phrase and Fable*.)

(227) My version has benefited from Nabokov's salutary, scholastic savaging of Robert Lowell's adaptation of this poem (*The New York Review of Books*, 4 December, 1969).

(258) 'The paintings he most likely had in mind were Monet's *Lilas au soleil* and Pissarro's *Boulevard Montmartre* and *Place du Théâtre Français, Printemps* (J. Baines).

Penultimate line: the Russian edition has 'murky [or gloomy] disorder' for 'sunny disorder'.

(from 267 and 268) My abbreviated version combines two poems on Ariosto. 'The manuscripts and drafts [of the first] were taken away when we were searched in May 1934. In Voronezh, O.M. tried to remember the text, but his memory failed him and he wrote a second *Ariosto*. Soon, on a trip to Moscow, I found the 1933 *Ariosto* in one of my hiding-places. So there were now two poems with the same theme and material. This is a story in the spirit of the times – and I present it to future commentators.' (N.M., from *Chapter 42*, translated by Donald Rayfield).

'the beard-shaver': Peter the Great learnt how to shave beards, pull teeth and chop off heads. Through Peter, O.M. is alluding to Stalin.

(286) The poem that led to O.M.'s first arrest, in 1934. As he said to N.M.: 'Above all, I detest . . . fascism.'

from *Journey to Armenia*: Akhmatova wondered how, in 1933, this passage got past the censor. In fact, the editor of *Star*, a Leningrad literary journal, disobeyed the censor; it cost him his job, but he was not arrested.

Arshak – O.M.; Shapukh – Stalin; Darmastat – Bukharin (executed 1938) who was O.M.'s protector and responsible for his being able to journey to Armenia.

(296) Lament inspired by O.M.'s contemplation of N.M.'s fate. In 1934 O.M. was arrested and spent two weeks in the Lubianka prison, where he was interrogated and tortured. As a supreme and miraculous act of clemency on the part of the 'Boss', he was sentenced to only three years exile; Stalin ordered that O.M. should be 'isolated but preserved.'

The rest of the poems in this book were composed in exile in Voronezh.

Of the Voronezh poems D. Rayfield has said: 'The poet as a thinker, as an incarnation of the Hellenic spirit, barely functions. He is only an eye bewildered by forests, rivers, earth, wooden houses, the open spaces and the boundless sky of the steppes, which itself seems to him to be an eye on a cosmic plane. His thoughts are paralysed by an instinctive feeling of a predator's presence, the Kremlin which is now the axis on which the poet's world rotates' ('Mandelstam's Voronezh poetry', *Russian Literature Triquarterly*, 1975); 'the poetry of 1933 and afterwards has a posthumous quality, breathing borrowed air on borrowed time' (*Grosseteste Review*, Vol. 7, Nos. 1-3. 'Deaths and Resurrections: The Later Poetry of Osip Mandelstam').

(306) Curvature, like that of the earth's surface, is a curious feature of Red Square, both as viewed from one side to the other, and also along the other axis, as it slopes down to the River Moskva. 'Red Square symbolises the rotten core of the system . . . [The] Stalinist Terror . . . knows no limits' (J. Baines).

(307) 'foot': 'the human and the metric foot which must both walk the black earth' (D. Rayfield).

'mumbling lips': 'the symbol of [his] poetry' (J. Baines).

(318) N.M. brought O.M. 'a souvenir of the past, a small bag of stones from Koktebel . . . [O.M.] affirms his predilection for the more prosaic pebbles from the sea' (J. Baines). There is an untranslatable pun in the second line: *opal* means 'opal', *opala* 'disgrace' in Russian.

(319) O.M. 'was beginning to see the soldiers as victims rather than oppressors, as vassals in the power of oriental-style despots, with their exotic retinues . . . of janissaries and eunuchs' (J. Baines).

'Lines on Stalin': O.M.'s 'positive' ode to Stalin. The original consists of seven twelve-line stanzas.

In January 1937, in exile, with the rope around his neck, O.M. tried to write an ode in praise of Stalin, to save his wife's life and his own. The attempt failed: this is part of the remarkably ambiguous result.

See *Slavic Review*, 1975; Bengt Jangfeldt: 'O.M.'s "Ode" to Stalin', *Scando-Slavica*, 1976; Clarence Brown: 'Into the Heart of Darkness: Mandelstam's Ode to Stalin', *Slavic Review*, 1967; and J. Baines: *Mandelstam: The Later Poetry*.

(350) 'The historical perspective which caused Mandelstam to see [Stalin] as the Judas not so much of present but of future generations was seldom achieved by his contemporaries in 1937, at the height of the Terror' (J. Baines).

(354) Third stanza, line 4: the 'shadow' Mandelshtam might have 'begged favour of' is Stalin.

(358) Henry Gifford (in a letter to me): 'The "stale loaves" suggest to me Dante's bread that tastes of salt, or what is called in *Richard II* "the bitter bread of banishment".'

(366) 'Urals': in 1934 Mandelshtam was exiled to the Urals, to Cherdyn (where – thinking he was going to be arrested again by the secret police – he threw himself out of the window of the hospital), and travelled along the Volga to arrive there.

'These steppes' refers to the area around Voronezh.

I am indebted to R. Chandler for drawing my attention to the fact that 'here are all my rights' refers to Pushkin's poem *From Piedmont* (1836), in which he says he doesn't mind about censorship, not having the right to vote, etc.; all he cares about is that he should be left to himself, not have to give account to others of what he does, and be free to wonder at the godlike beauties of nature and art: 'Here is my happiness! Here are my rights . . .'

R. F. Holmes has pointed out to me that 'of course both poets *did* care about other things than being left to themselves . . . Mandelshtam, besides attacking Stalin, attacked one Caesar at least, two Tsars, Napoleon, Hitler and Mussolini.' (In *Rome*, composed in 1937, Rome is characterised as a 'nursery for murder'; 'The degenerate chin of the dictator/Sags over Rome').

(367) This poem was written during the time when Mandelshtam was particularly obsessed with Joseph Stalin. Wasp, in Russian, is *osa*, axis is *os'*. Joseph, in Russian, can be either *Os*ip or *Ios*if.

O.M. 'obviously listed here some of the arts officially . . . encouraged in the mid-thirties, the period of violin-competitions, portrait-painting, the revival of the classical opera . . .' (O. Ronen, *An Approach to Mandelstam*).

(368) The last poem in Mandelshtam's Stalin cycle. Scythe, in Russian, is 'kosa'. The cuckoo, as also in 'the cuckoo is weeping in its stone tower' (No. 121), alludes to a passage from *The Lay of Igor's Campaign*, a twelfth-century poem in which Yaroslavna, Igor's wife, mourns him 'like a desolate cuckoo'. 'On the Danube Yaroslavna's voice is heard: like a desolate cuckoo she cries early in the morning. "I will fly," she says, "like a cuckoo along the Danube, I will dip my sleeve of beaver-fur in the river Kayala, I will wipe the Prince's bleeding wounds . . ."' (*Penguin Book of Russian Verse*, edited by D. Obolensky). '[Mandelstam] lamented his failing eyesight, which had once been "sharper than a whetted scythe" but had not had time to pick out each of the "lonely multitude of stars".' (N.M., *Hope Against Hope*.)

(370) 'Speaking of himself, he used here the "inexorable past tense" . . . A

105

few more months were to pass, and he would say to Akhmatova: "I am ready for death".' (N.M., *Hope Against Hope*.)

Here O.M., according to D. Rayfield, sees himself as Daniel who championed Israel (*Russian Literature Triquarterly*, 1975).

'the singer is free to descend into the lion's den, since her voice can conquer the lion, escape from the fortress – Marian Anderson's speciality was negro spirituals . . .' (J. Baines).

The poem combines two images: of Marian Anderson, whose deep voice O.M. had heard on the radio; and of a singer friend whose husband had just been re-arrested after recent release from five years in a camp. (See *Hope Against Hope*, chapter 39.)

(384) N.M., the 'child' or 'little one', is entrusted in this lullaby and love poem to the care of the stars because 'the radiance of the stars is also that of his poetry' (J. Baines).

O.M. was embarrassed, as far as eventual publication might be concerned, by the intimacy of what he called 'these verses of the bed'.

(385) Line 8: 'Presumably this means that the pot split into the two aspects of poetry: the raw material – the sea which gave birth to Aphrodite – and the forming, shaping poetic eye' (D. Rayfield, private communication).

'. . . Hera was first worshipped in the form of a cow' (J. Baines).

(387) 'The Greek flute's sounds are clearly the poetic force before it has been precipitated in language . . . [The] flute's music . . . crosses barriers, it is unselfconscious . . . The poet creates his own past; "making his native sea" out of clay, like the Cretan potters . . . [But] the flautist is in the past, unrepeatable. He is what the poet might have been or continued being, had the Hellenic world not fallen apart. Now nothing works: the sea gives no birth . . . [it] kills instead of giving life . . . [Mandelshtam's] lips cannot work the flute, and the balance of forces . . . topples, leaving only the destructive, negative force to silence poetry . . . If there is a moral in the poem, it is that the poet, conscious of his individual death, is tainted by his fear and loses his gift of immersing himself in the medium of poetry.' (D. Rayfield, *Russian Literature Triquarterly*, 1975).

Rayfield points out that *sea* (*more*) changes into its phonetic twin *plague* (*mor*) – which I have rendered as *disease*; similarly the 'syllable *ub* joins the flautist's mouth (*zuby*, teeth, and *guby*, lips) in a fatal conjunction with death (*ub*iystvo, murder . . .). – This sort of thing, of course, drives the translator to despair, if not self-destruction.

N.M. writes about this poem in *Hope against Hope*, chapter 39: 'Since he works with his voice, a poet's lips are the tools of his trade, and in . . . [this] poem O.M. is also speaking about his own whispering lips and the painful process of converting into words the sounds ringing in his ears . . . The poem is . . . about a flute player we knew . . . He would bring great comfort to O.M. by playing Bach or Schubert for him. Schwab . . . [was] accused of espionage and sent to a camp for common criminals . . . He was already an old man and he ended his days there.'

(388) Henry Gifford discusses an early poem by Pasternak where the latter mentions 'sticky greenery' which seems to evoke the 'sticky little leaves opening in spring' that reconciled Ivan Karamazov to life' (Henry Gifford, *Pasternak*).

(394) The limping woman was Natasha Shtempel, whom the Mandelshtams knew in Voronezh.

Acknowledgements

Passages from the following works are quoted in the Notes by permission:

Jennifer Baines, *Mandelstam: the Later Poetry* (Cambridge Univ. Press, 1976).

Clarence Brown, *Mandelstam* (Cambridge University Press, London and New York, 1973).

Steven Broyde, *Osip Mandelstam and his Age* (Harvard Univ. Press, 1975).

Peter France, *Poets of Modern Russia* (Cambridge University Press, 1982).

Henry Gifford, *Pasternak* (Cambridge University Press, 1977).

Poetry in a Divided World (Cambridge University Press, 1986).

Nadezhda Mandelstam, *Hope Against Hope* and *Hope Abandoned* (Copyright © 1970 and Copyright © 1972 respectively by Atheneum Publishers; English translation Copyright © 1970 and Copyright © 1973, 1974 respectively by Atheneum Publishers, New York and Harvill Press Ltd., London; published by Atheneum publishers, New York and William Collins & Harvill Press, London.

Chapter 42 and Osip Mandelstam, *'The Goldfinch' and other poems*, translated with an introduction by Donald Rayfield (The Menard Press, 1973).

Osip Mandelstam, *Complete Critical Prose and Letters*, edited by Jane Gary Harris, trans. by Jane Gary Harris and Constance Link (Ardis, 1979).

Osip Mandelstam: Selected Essays, translated and edited with an introduction by Sidney Monas (University of Texas Press, 1977).

Osip Mandelstam's 'Stone', translated with an introduction by Robert Tracy (Princeton University Press, 1981).

Sidney Monas, notes to *Complete Poetry of Osip Mandelstam*, translated by Burton Raffel and Alla Burago (by permission of the State University of New York Press; Copyright © 1973 State University of New York).

N. A. Nilsson, *Osip Mandelstam: Five Poems* (Almqvist & Wiksell International, Stockholm, 1974).

The Penguin Book of Russian Verse, introduced and edited by Dimitri Obolensky (Copyright © Dimitri Obolensky, 1962, 1963; published by Penguin Books).

Omry Ronen, *An Approach to Mandelstam* (The Magnes Press, The Hebrew University, Jerusalem, 1983).

Tom Stableford, *The Literary Appreciation of Russian Writers* (Cambridge University Press, 1981).

Kiril Taranovsky, *Essays on Mandelstam* (Harvard University Press, 1976).

Further Reading:
A Select Bibliography

BOOKS

Baines, Jennifer, *Mandelstam: The Later Poetry*, Cambridge University Press, 1976.

Blot, Jean, *Osip Mandelshtam*, Poètes d'aujourd'hui 206, Seghers, Paris, 1972.

Broyde, S., *Osip Mandelstam and his Age: War and Revolution in the poetry 1913-1923*, Harvard Slavic Monographs 1, 1975.

Brown, Clarence *(translation)*, *The Prose of Osip Mandelstam*, North Point Press, Berkeley, CA; Quartet, London, 1967.

Mandelstam. Cambridge University Press, 1973.

Cohen, Arthur A., *O. E. Mandelshtam. An essay in Antiphon*, Ardis, Ann Arbor, Michigan, 1974.

Freidin, Grigory, *A Coat of Many Colours,*, Berkeley, CA, 1988.

Isenberg, Charles, *Substantial Proofs of Being: Osip Mandelstam's Literary Prose*, Slavica, Ohio, 1987.

Harris, Jane Gary *(translation and introduction)*, *Mandelstam: The Complete Critical Prose and Letters*. Ardis, Ann Arbor, Michigan, 1979.

Osip Mandelstam, Twayne, Boston, 1988.

Koubourlis, Dimitri, *A Concordance to the poems of Osip Mandelshtam*, Cornell University Press, Ithaca and London, 1974.

Mandelstam, Nadezhda Yakovlevna, *Hope against Hope*, Atheneum, New York and Collins and Harvill, London, 1976.

Hope Abandoned, Atheneum, New York and Collins and Harvill, London, 1973.

Mozart and Salieri. An essay on Osip Mandelstam and Poetic Creativity, Ardis, Ann Arbor, Michigan, 1973.

Monas, Sydney *(translation and introduction)*, *Osip Mandelstam: Selected Essays*, University of Texas, Austin, 1977.

Nilsson, Nils Åke, *Osip Mandel'štam: Five Poems*, Uppsala, 1974.

Przybylski, Ryszard, *An essay on the poetry of Osip Mandelstam: God's Grateful Guest*. Ardis, Ann Arbor, Michigan, 1987.

Rayfield, Donald *(introduction and translations)*, Nadezhda Mandel'shtam, *Chapter 42*, and Osip Mandel'shtam, *'The Goldfinch' and other poems*, The Menard Press, London, 1973.

Ronen, Omry, *An Approach to Mandelshtam*, Slavica Hierosolymitana, The Magnes Press, Jerusalem, 1983.

Struve, Nikita, *Ossip Mandelstam*, Institut d'Études Slaves, Paris, 1982,

Taranovsky, Kiril, *Essays on Mandel'štam*, Harvard University Press, Cambridge, Mass. and London, 1976.

Tracy, Robert *(translation and introduction)*, *Osip Mandelstam's 'Stone'*, Princeton University Press, N.J. and Guildford, Surrey, 1981.

West, Daphne M., *Mandelstam: The Egyptian Stamp*, Birmingham Slavonic Monographs No. 10, University of Birmingham, 1980.

Zeeman, Peter, *The Later Poetry of Osip Mandelstam: Text and Context*, Rodopi, Amsterdam, 1988.

ARTICLES

Bodin, Per-Arne, 'Understanding the sign. An analysis of 'Sredi svyashchennikov . . .' *Scando-Slavica*, Stockholm, 31, 1985, pp. 31-39.

Brown, Clarence, 'Into the Heart of Darkness: Mandelstam's Ode to Stalin', *Slavic Review*, Stanford, CA, December 1967, pp. 584-604.

'Mandelstam's Notes towards a Supreme Fiction', *Delos*, Austin, Texas, 1968, pp. 32-48.

Brown, Clarence and Hughes, Robert *(translators)*, 'Mandelstam: Talking about Dante', *Delos*, 6, 1971.

Freidin, Grigory, 'The whisper of history and the noise of time in the writings of Osip Mandelstam', *Russian Review*, XXXVII/4 Columbus, OH, October 1978, pp. 421-37.

Harris, Jane Gary, 'The "Latin Gerundive" as Autobiographical Imperative: A Reading of Mandelshtam's Journey to Armenia', *Slavic Review*, 45, 1986, pp. 1-19.

Monas, Sidney *(translation and introduction)*, *Osip Mandelstam: Journey to Armenia*, George F. Ritchie, San Francisco, 1979.

Nilsson, Nils Åke, 'Osip Mandelshtam and his Poetry', *Scando-Slavica*, IV, 1963, pp. 37-59.

'To Kassandra. A poem by Osip Mandelshtam', *Poetica Slavica*, Ottawa, 1981, pp. 39-49.

Rayfield, Donald, 'The Flight from Chaos', *European Judaism*, Amsterdam, 1971-72, pp. 37-41.

'A Winter in Moscow (Osip Mandelshtam's poems of 1933-34)', *Stand*, Newcastle upon Tyne, XIV/1, 1972, pp. 18-23.

'Deaths and Resurrections', *Grosseteste Review*, Lincoln, VII/1-3, 1974, pp. 156-77.

'Mandelshtam: The Voronezh Notebooks', *Russian Literature Triquarterly*, Ann Arbor, Michigan, 11, 1975, pp. 323-62.

'Lamarck and Mandelshtam', *Scottish Slavonic Review*, Glasgow, 9, autumn 1987, pp. 85-101.

Struve, Nikita, 'Les thèmes chrétiens dans l'oeuvre d'Osip Mandelstam', *Essays in honor of Georges Florovsky*, II: *The religious world of Russian culture. Russia and Orthodoxy*, Mouton, Amsterdam, 1975, pp. 305-13.

Terras, Victor, 'Classical Motives in the Poetry of Mandelstam', *Slavic and East European Journal*, Quebec, X/3, 1966, pp. 251-67.

'The time philosophy of Mandelstam', *Slavonic and East European Review*, London, XLVII, 1969, pp. 344-54.

Vitins, Ieva, 'Mandelshtam's Farewell to Marina Tsvetaeva', *Slavic Review*, XLVI/2, 1987, pp. 266-80.

Zeeman, Peter, 'Reference and interpretation (Mandelstam)', *Russian Literature*, Amsterdam, XVIII, 1985, pp. 257-98.

'Irony in Mandelstam's later poetry', *Russian Literature*, XIX, 1986, pp. 405-44.

'Metaphorical language in Mandelstam', *Russian Literature*, XXI, 1987, pp. 313-46.

APPENDIX:

*Russian texts of poems
translated*

The following texts are printed, by permission, by photographic reproduction from Osip Mandelshtam, *Sobraniye sochineniy* (Collected Works), edited by G. P. Struve and B. A. Filippov, Inter-Language Literary Associates, second edition revised and expanded, Vol. I, Washington, 1967; except for two passages from Vol. II of this edition – the unnumbered stanza on page 113 (Gleb/Struve no. 457Z) and the excerpt from *Journey to Armenia* (page 131) – and 'Stikhi o Staline' ('Lines on Stalin', page 133), printed from the text published in *Scando-Slavica*, Stockholm, Tomus 22, 1976.

1.

Звук осторожный и глухой
Плода, сорвавшегося с древа,
Среди немолчного напева
Глубокой тишины лесной . . .

3.

Из полутемной залы, вдруг,
Ты выскользнула в легкой шали —
Мы никому не помешали,
Мы не будили спящих слуг . . .

4.

Только детские книги читать,
Только детские думы лелеять,
Все большое далеко развеять,
Из глубокой печали восстать.

Я от жизни смертельно устал,
Ничего от нее не приемлю,
Но люблю мою бедную землю
Оттого, что иной не видал.

Я качался в далеком саду
На простой деревянной качели,
И высокие темные ели
Вспоминаю в туманном бреду.

6.

На бледно-голубой эмали,
Какая мыслима в апреле,
Березы ветви поднимали
И незаметно вечерели.

Узор отточенный и мелкий,
Застыла тоненькая сетка,
Как на фарфоровой тарелке
Рисунок, вычерченный метко,

Когда его художник милый
Выводит на стеклянной тверди,
В сознании минутной силы,
В забвении печальной смерти.

8.

Дано мне тело — что мне делать с ним,
Таким единым и таким моим?

За радость тихую дышать и жить,
Кого, скажите, мне благодарить?

Я и садовник, я же и цветок,
В темнице мира я не одинок.

На стекла вечности уже легло
Мое дыхание, мое тепло.

Запечатлеется на нем узор,
Неузнаваемый с недавних пор.

Пускай мгновения стекает муть —
Узора милого не зачеркнуть.

9.

Невыразимая печаль
Открыла два огромных глаза,
Цветочная проснулась ваза
И выплеснула свой хрусталь.

Вся комната напоена
Истомой — сладкое лекарство!
Такое маленькое царство
Так много поглотило сна.

Немного красного вина,
Немного солнечного мая —
И, тоненький бисквит ломая,
Тончайших пальцев белизна.

*

Колосья, так недавно сжаты,
Рядами ровными лежат;
И пальцы тонкие дрожат,
К таким же, как они, прижаты.

11.

Ни о чем не нужно говорить,
Ничему не следует учить,
И печальна так и хороша
Темная звериная душа:

Ничему не хочет научить,
Не умеет вовсе говорить
И плывет дельфином молодым
По седым пучинам мировым.

14. SILENTIUM

Она еще не родила́сь,
Она и музыка и слово,
И потому всего живого
Ненаруша́емая связь.

Спокойно дыша́т моря́ груди,
Но, как безумный, светел день,
И пе́ны бледная сирень
В мутно-лазоревом сосу́де.

Да обретут мои уста́
Первоначальную немоту,
Как кристаллическую ноту,
Что от рождения чиста́!

Останься пеной, Афродита,
И слово в музыку вернись,
И сердце сердца устыдись,
С первоосновой жизни сли́то!

15.

Слух чуткий парус напрягает,
Расширенный пустеет взор
И тишину переплывает
Полночных птиц незвучный хор.

Я так же беден как природа
И так же прост как небеса,
И призрачна моя свобода,
Как птиц полночных голоса.

Я вижу месяц бездыханный
И небо мертвенней холста;
Твой мир болезненный и странный
Я принимаю, пустота!

16.

Как тень внезапных облаков,
Морская гостья налетела
И, проскользнув, прошелестела
Смущенных мимо берегов.

Огромный парус строго реет;
Смертельно-бледная волна
Отпрянула — и вновь она
Коснуться берега не смеет;

И лодка, волнами шурша,
Как листьями . . .

17.

Из омута злого и вязкого
Я вырос, тростинкой шурша,
И страстно, и томно, и ласково
Запретною жизнью дыша.

И никну, никем не замеченный,
В холодный и топкий приют,
Приветственным шелестом встреченный
Коротких осенних минут.

Я счастлив жестокой обидою
И в жизни, похожей на сон,
Я каждому тайно завидую
И в каждого тайно влюблен.

19.

Душный сумрак кроет ложе,
Напряженно дышет грудь . . .
Может, мне всего дороже
Тонкий крест и тайный путь.

20.

Как кони медленно ступают,
Как мало в фонарях огня!
Чужие люди, верно, знают,
Куда везут они меня.

А я вверяюсь их заботе,
Мне холодно, я спать хочу;
Подбросило на повороте
Навстречу звездному лучу.

Горячей головы качанье
И нежный лед руки чужой,
И темных елей очертанья,
Еще невиданные мной.

21.

Скудный луч холодной мерою
Сеет свет в сыром лесу.
Я печаль, как птицу серую,
В сердце медленно несу.

Что мне делать с птицей раненой?
Твердь умолкла, умерла.
С колокольни отуманенной
Кто-то снял колокола,

114

И стоит осиротелая
И немая вышина,
Как пустая башня белая,
Где туман и тишина.

Утро, нежностью бездонное,
Полуявь и полусон —
Забытье неутоленное —
Дум туманный перезвон . . .

26. РАКОВИНА

Быть может, я тебе не нужен,
Ночь; из пучины мировой,
Как раковина без жемчужин,
Я выброшен на берег твой.

Ты равнодушно волны пенишь
И несговорчиво поешь;
Но ты полюбишь, ты оценишь
Ненужной раковины ложь.

Ты на песок с ней рядом ляжешь,
Оденешь ризою своей,
Ты неразрывно с нею свяжешь
Огромный колокол зыбей;

И хрупкой раковины стены,
Как нежилого сердца дом,
Наполнишь шопотами пены,
Туманом, ветром и дождем . . .

29.

Я ненавижу свет
Однообразных звезд.
Здравствуй, мой давний бред —
Башни стрельчатой рост!

Кружевом, камень, будь,
И паутиной стань:
Неба пустую грудь
Тонкой иглою рань.

Будет и мой черед —
Чую размах крыла.
Так — но куда уйдет
Мысли живой стрела?

Или, свой путь и срок
Я, исчерпав, вернусь:
Там — я любить не мог,
Здесь — я любить боюсь . . .

30.

Образ твой, мучительный и зыбкий,
Я не мог в тумане осязать.
«Господи!» — сказал я по ошибке,
Сам того не думая сказать.

Божье имя, как большая птица,
Вылетело из моей груди.
Впереди густой туман клубится,
И пустая клетка позади.

31.

Нет, не луна, а светлый циферблат
Сияет мне, и чем я виноват,
Что слабых звезд я осязаю млечность?

И Батюшкова мне противна спесь:
«Который час?» его спросили здесь,
А он ответил любопытным: «вечность».

32. ПЕШЕХОД

Я чувствую непобедимый страх
В присутствии таинственных высот,
Я ласточкой доволен в небесах
И колокольни я люблю полет!

И, кажется, старинный пешеход,
Над пропастью, на гнущихся мостках
Я слушаю, как снежный ком растет
И вечность бьет на каменных часах.

Когда бы так! Но я не путник тот,
Мелькающий на выцветших листвах,
И подлинно во мне печаль поет;

Действительно, лавина есть в горах!
И вся моя душа — в колоколах,
Но музыка от бездны не спасет!

33. КАЗИНО

Я не поклонник радости предвзятой,
Подчас природа — серое пятно.
Мне, в опьяненьи легком, суждено
Изведать краски жизни небогатой.

Играет ветер тучею косматой,
Ложится якорь на морское дно,
И бездыханная, как полотно,
Душа висит над бездною проклятой.

Но я люблю на дюнах казино,
Широкий вид в туманное окно
И тонкий луч на скатерти измятой;

И, окружен водой зеленоватой,
Когда, как роза, в хрустале вино —
Люблю следить за чайкою крылатой!

37. ЛЮТЕРАНИН

Я на прогулке похороны встретил
Близ протестантской кирки, в воскресенье.
Рассеянный прохожий, я заметил
Тех прихожан суровое волненье.

Чужая речь не достигала слуха,
И только упряжь тонкая сияла,
Да мостовая праздничная глухо
Ленивые подковы отражала.

А в эластичном сумраке кареты,
Куда печаль забилась, лицемерка,
Без слов, без слез, скупая на приветы,
Осенних роз мелькнула бутоньерка.

Тянулись иностранцы лентой черной,
И шли пешком заплаканные дамы,
Румянец под вуалью, и упорно
Над ними кучер правил в даль, упрямый.

Кто б ни был ты, покойный лютеранин, —
Тебя легко и просто хоронили.
Был взор слезой приличной затуманен,
И сдержанно колокола звонили.

И думал я: витийствовать не надо.
Мы не пророки, даже не предтечи,
Не любим рая, не боимся ада,
И в полдень матовый горим, как свечи.

38. АЙЯ-СОФИЯ

Айя-София — здесь остановиться
Судил Господь народам и царям!
Ведь купол твой, по слову очевидца,
Как на цепи подвешен к небесам.

И всем векам — пример Юстиниана,
Когда похитить для чужих богов
Позволила Эфесская Диана
Сто семь зеленых мраморных столбов.

Но что же думал твой строитель щедрый,
Когда, душой и помыслом высок,
Расположил апсиды и экседры,
Им указав на запад и восток?

Прекрасен храм, купающийся в мире,
И сорок окон — света торжество;
На парусах, под куполом, четыре
Архангела прекраснее всего.

И мудрое сферическое зданье
Народы и века переживет,
И серафимов гулкое рыданье
Не покоробит темных позолот.

39. NOTRE DAME

Где римский судия судил чужой народ —
Стоит базилика, и радостный и первый,
Как некогда Адам, распластывая нервы,
Играет мышцами крестовый легкий свод.

Но выдает себя снаружи тайный план:
Здесь позаботилась подпружных арок сила,
Чтоб масса грузная стены не сокрушила,
И свода дерзкого бездействует таран.

Стихийный лабиринт, непостижимый лес,
Души готической рассудочная пропасть,
Египетская мощь и христианства робость,
С тростинкой рядом — дуб, и всюду царь —
                                        отвес.

Но чем внимательней, твердыня Notre Dame,
Я изучал твои чудовищные ребра,
Тем чаще думал я: из тяжести недоброй
И я когда-нибудь прекрасное создам.

116

54.

Отравлен хлеб и воздух выпит.
Как трудно раны врачевать!
Иосиф, проданный в Египет,
Не мог сильнее тосковать!

Под звездным небом бедуины,
Закрыв глаза и на коне,
Слагают вольные былины
О смутно пережитом дне.

Немного нужно для наитий:
Кто потерял в песке колчан,
Кто выменял коня — событий
Рассеивается туман;

И если подлинно поется
И полной грудью — наконец
Всё исчезает: остается
Пространство, звезды и певец!

60.

О временах простых и грубых
Копыта конские твердят.
И дворники в тяжелых шубах
На деревянных лавках спят.

На стук в железные ворота
Привратник, царственно-ленив,

Встал, и звериная зевота
Напомнила твой образ, скиф!

Когда, с дряхлеющей любовью
Мешая в песнях Рим и снег,
Овидий пел арбу воловью
В походе варварских телег.

62.

Есть иволги в лесах, и гласных долгота
В тонических стихах единственная мера.
Но только раз в году бывает разлита
В природе длительность, как в метрике Гомера.

Как бы цезурою зияет этот день:
Уже с утра покой и трудные длинноты;
Волы на пастбище, и золотая лень
Из тростника извлечь богатство целой ноты.

65.

Природа — тот же Рим и отразилась в нем.
Мы видим образы его гражданской мощи
В прозрачном воздухе, как в цирке голубом,
На форуме полей и в колоннаде рощи.

Природа — тот же Рим, и, кажется, опять
Нам незачем богов напрасно беспокоить:
Есть внутренности жертв, чтоб о войне гадать,
Рабы, чтобы молчать, и камни, чтобы строить!

78.

Бессонница. Гомер. Тугие паруса.
Я список кораблей прочел до середины:
Сей длинный выводок, сей поезд журавлиный,
Что над Элладою когда-то поднялся.

Как журавлиный клин в чужие рубежи —
На головах царей божественная пена —
Куда плывете вы? Когда бы не Елена,
Что Троя вам одна, ахейские мужи?

И море, и Гомер — всё движется любовью.
Кого же слушать мне? И вот Гомер молчит,
И море черное, витийствуя, шумит
И с тяжким грохотом подходит к изголовью.

80.

С веселым ржанием пасутся табуны,
И римской ржавчиной окрасилась долина;
Сухое золото классической весны
Уносит времени прозрачная стремнина.

Топча по осени дубовые листы,
Что густо стелются пустынною тропинкой,
Я вспомню Цезаря прекрасные черты —
Сей профиль женственный с коварною горбинкой!

Здесь, Капитолия и Форума вдали,
Средь увядания спокойного природы,
Я слышу Августа и на краю земли
Державным яблоком катящиеся годы.

Да будет в старости печаль моя светла:
Я в Риме родился, и он ко мне вернулся;
Мне осень добрая волчицею была
И — месяц цезарей — мне август улыбнулся.

165.

Заманили охотники в капкан:
По тебе будут плакать леса, олень!

Солнце, возьми мой черный плащ,
Но сохрани живую мощь!

178.

Как овцы, жалкою толпой
Бежали старцы Еврипида.
Иду змеиною тропой
И в сердце темная обида.

Но этот час уж недалек:
Я отряхну мои печали,
Как мальчик вечером песок
Вытряхивает из сандалий.

— Как этих покрывал и этого убора
Мне пышность тяжела средь моего позора!

    — Будет в каменной Трезене
    Знаменитая беда,
    Царской лестницы ступени
    Покраснеют от стыда,

    . . . .

    И для матери влюбленной
    Солнце черное взойдет.

— О если б ненависть в груди моей кипела —
Но видите — само признанье с уст слетело.

    — Черным пламенем Федра горит
    Среди белого дня.
    Погребальный факел чадит
    Среди белого дня.
    Бойся матери ты, Ипполит:
    Федра — ночь — тебя сторожит
    Среди белого дня.

— Любовью черною я солнце запятнала . . .
. . . .

    — Мы боимся, мы не смеем
    Горю царскому помочь.
    Уязвленная Тезеем
    На него напала ночь.
    Мы же, песнью похоронной

    Провожая мертвых в дом,
    Страсти дикой и бессонной
    Солнце черное уймем.

В Петрополе прозрачном мы умрем,
Где властвует над нами Прозерпина.
Мы в каждом вздохе смертный воздух пьем,
И каждый час нам смертная година.
Богиня моря, грозная Афина,
Сними могучий каменный шелом.
В Петрополе прозрачном мы умрем,
Где царствуешь не ты, а Прозерпина.

    Эта ночь непоправима,
    А у вас еще светло.
    У ворот Ерусалима
    Солнце черное взошло.

Солнце желтое страшнее —
Баю баюшки баю —
В светлом храме иудеи
Хоронили мать мою.

Благодати не имея
И священства лишены,
В светлом храме иудеи
Отпевали прах жены.

И над матерью звенели
Голоса израильтян.
Я проснулся в колыбели,
Черным солнцем осиян.

Не веря воскресенья чуду,
На кладбище гуляли мы.
— Ты знаешь, мне земля повсюду
Напоминает те холмы

. . . .

Где обрывается Россия
Над морем черным и глухим.

От монастырских косогоров
Широкий убегает луг.
Мне от владимирских просторов
Так не хотелося на юг,
Но в этой темной, деревянной
И юродивой слободе
С такой монашкою туманной
Остаться — значит быть беде.

Целую локоть загорелый
И лба кусочек восковой.
Я знаю — он остался белый
Под смуглой прядью золотой.
Целую кисть, где от браслета
Еще белеет полоса.
Навриды пламенное лето
Творит такие чудеса.

Как скоро ты смуглянкой стала
И к Спасу бедному пришла,
Не отрываясь целовала,
А гордою в Москве была.
Нам остается только имя —
Чудесный звук, на долгий срок.
Прими ж ладонями моими
Пересыпаемый песок.

Золотистого меда струя из бутылки текла
Так тягуче и долго, что молвить хозяйка успела:
Здесь, в печальной Тавриде, куда нас судьба занесла,
Мы совсем не скучаем — и через плечо поглядела.

Всюду Бахуса службы, как будто на свете одни
Сторожа и собаки — идешь, никого не заметишь —
Как тяжелые бочки, спокойные катятся дни:
Далеко в шалаше голоса — не поймешь, не ответишь.

После чаю мы вышли в огромный коричневый сад,
Как ресницы на окнах опущены темные шторы,
Мимо белых колонн мы пошли посмотреть виноград,
Где воздушным стеклом обливаются сонные горы.

Я сказал: виноград как старинная битва живет,
Где курчавые всадники бьются в кудрявом порядке.
В каменистой Тавриде наука Эллады — и вот
Золотых десятин благородные, ржавые грядки.

Ну, а в комнате белой как прялка стоит тишина.
Пахнет уксусом, краской и свежим вином из подвала.
Помнишь, в греческом доме: любимая всеми жена —
Не Елена — другая — как долго она вышивала?

Золотое руно, где же ты, золотое руно?
Всю дорогу шумели морские тяжелые волны,
И покинув корабль, натрудивший в морях полотно,
Одиссей возвратился, пространством и временем полный.

___

93.

Еще далеко асфоделей
Прозрачно-серая весна.
Пока еще на самом деле
Шуршит песок, кипит волна.
Но здесь душа моя вступает,
Как Персефона, в легкий круг,
И в царстве мертвых не бывает
Прелестных загорелых рук.

Зачем же лодке доверяем
Мы тяжесть урны гробовой,
И праздник черных роз свершаем
Над аметистовой водой?
Туда душа моя стремится,
За мыс туманный Меганом,
И черный парус возвратится
Оттуда после похорон!

Как быстро тучи пробегают
Неосвещенною грядой,
И хлопья черных роз летают
Под этой ветряной луной.
И, птица смерти и рыданья,
Влачится траурной каймой
Огромный флаг воспоминанья
За кипарисною кормой.

И раскрывается с шуршаньем
Печальный веер прошлых лет,
Туда, где с темным содроганьем
В песок зарылся амулет;
Туда душа моя стремится,
За мыс туманный Меганом,
И черный парус возвратится
Оттуда после похорон!

Я изучил науку расставанья
В простоволосых жалобах ночных.
Жуют волы, и длится ожиданье,
Последний час вигилий городских,
И чту обряд той петушиной ночи,
Когда, подняв дорожной скорби груз,
Глядели вдаль заплаканные очи,
И женский плач мешался с пеньем муз.

Кто может знать при слове — расставанье,
Какая нам разлука предстоит,
Что нам сулит петушье восклицанье,
Когда огонь в акрополе горит,
И на заре какой-то новой жизни,
Когда в сенях лениво вол жует,
Зачем петух, глашатай новой жизни,
На городской стене крылами бьет?

И я люблю обыкновенье пряжи:
Снует челнок, веретено жужжит,
Смотри, навстречу, словно пух лебяжий,
Уже босая Делия летит!
О, нашей жизни скудная основа,
Куда как беден радости язык!
Всё было встарь, всё повторится снова,
И сладок нам лишь узнаванья миг.

Да будет так: прозрачная фигурка
На чистом блюде глиняном лежит,
Как беличья распластанная шкурка,
Склонясь над воском, девушка глядит.
Не нам гадать о греческом Эребе,
Для женщин воск, что для мужчины медь.
Нам только в битвах выпадает жребий,
А им дано гадая умереть.

108.

Сестры — тяжесть и нежность — одинаковы
                                ваши приметы.
Медуницы и осы тяжелую розу сосут.
Человек умирает, песок остывает согретый,
И вчерашнее солнце на черных носилках несут.

Ах, тяжелые соты и нежные сети,
Легче камень поднять, чем имя твое повторить!
У меня остается одна забота на свете:
Золотая забота, как времени бремя избыть.

Словно темную воду я пью помутившийся воздух.
Время вспахано плугом, и роза землею была.
В медленном водовороте тяжелые нежные розы,
Розы тяжесть и нежность в двойные венки заплела.

109.

Вернись в смесительное лоно,
Откуда, Лия, ты пришла,
За то, что солнцу Илиона
Ты желтый сумрак предпочла.

Иди, никто тебя не тронет,
На грудь отца в глухую ночь
Пускай главу свою уронит
Кровосмесительница-дочь.

Но роковая перемена
В тебе исполниться должна:
Ты будешь Лия — не Елена, —
Не потому наречена,

Что царской крови тяжелее
Струиться в жилах, чем другой —
Нет, ты полюбишь иудея,
Исчезнешь в нем — и Бог с тобой.

112.

Когда Психея-жизнь спускается к теням
В полупрозрачный лес, вослед за Персефоной,
Слепая ласточка бросается к ногам
С стигийской нежностью и веткою зеленой.

Навстречу беженке спешит толпа теней,
Товарку новую встречая причитаньем,
И руки слабые ломают перед ней
С недоуменьем и робким упованьем.

Кто держит зеркало, кто баночку духов —
Душа ведь женщина, — ей нравятся безделки,
И лес безлиственный прозрачных голосов
Сухие жалобы кропят, как дождик мелкий.

И в нежной сутолке не зная, что начать,
Душа не узнает прозрачные дубравы;
Дохнет на зеркало, и медлит передать
Лепешку медную с туманной переправы.

113.

Я слово позабыл, что я хотел сказать.
Слепая ласточка в чертог теней вернется,
На крыльях срезанных, с прозрачными
                                играть.
В беспамятстве ночная песнь поется.

Не слышно птиц. Бессмертник не цветет.
Прозрачны гривы табуна ночного.
В сухой реке пустой челнок плывет.
Среди кузнечиков беспамятствует слово.

И медленно растет, как бы шатер иль храм,
То вдруг прокинется безумной Антигоной,
То мертвой ласточкой бросается к ногам
С стигийской нежностью и веткою зеленой.

О если бы вернуть и зрячих пальцев стыд,
И выпуклую радость узнаванья.
Я так боюсь рыданья Аонид,
Тумана, звона и зиянья.

А смертным власть дана любить и узнавать,
Для них и звук в персты прольется,
Но я забыл, что я хочу сказать,
И мысль бесплотная в чертог теней вернется.

Всё не о том прозрачная твердит,
Всё ласточка, подружка, Антигона ...
А на губах как черный лед горит
Стигийского воспоминанье звона.

116.

Возьми на радость из моих ладоней
Немного солнца и немного меда,
Как нам велели пчелы Персефоны.

Не отвязать неприкрепленной лодки,
Не услыхать в меха обутой тени,
Не превозмочь в дремучей жизни страха.

Нам остаются только поцелуи,
Мохнатые, как маленькие пчелы,
Что умирают, вылетев из улья.

Они шуршат в прозрачных дебрях ночи,
Их родина — дремучий лес Тайгета,
Их пища — время, медуница, мята.

Возьми ж на радость дикий мой подарок,
Невзрачное сухое ожерелье
Из мертвых пчел, мед превративших в солнце.

117.

Вот дароносица, как солнце золотое,
Повисла в воздухе — великолепный миг,
Здесь должен прозвучать лишь греческий язык:
Взять в руки целый мир, как яблоко простое.

Богослужения торжественный зенит,
Свет в круглой храмине под куполом в июле,
Чтоб полной грудью мы вне времени вздохнули
О луговине той, где время не бежит.

И Евхаристия как вечный полдень длится —
Все причащаются, играют и поют,
И на виду у всех божественный сосуд
Неисчерпаемым весельем струится.

119.

За то, что я руки твои не сумел удержать,
За то, что я предал соленые нежные губы,
Я должен рассвета в дремучем акрополе ждать.
Как я ненавижу плакучие древние срубы.

Ахейские мужи во тьме снаряжают коня,
Зубчатыми пилами в стены вгрызаются крепко,
Никак не уляжется крови сухая возня,
И нет для тебя ни названья, ни звука, ни слепка.

Как мог я подумать, что ты возвратишься, как смел!
Зачем преждевременно я от тебя оторвался!
Еще не рассеялся мрак и петух не пропел,
Еще в древесину горячий топор не врезался.

Прозрачной слезой на стенах проступила смола,
И чувствует город свои деревянные ребра,
Но хлынула к лестницам кровь и на приступ пошла,
И трижды приснился мужам соблазнительный образ.

Где милая Троя? где царский, где девичий дом?
Он будет разрушен, высокий Приамов скворешник.
И падают стрелы сухим деревянным дождем,
И стрелы другие растут на земле, как орешник.

Последней звезды безболезненно гаснет укол,
И серою ласточкой утро в окно постучится,
И медленный день, как в соломе проснувшийся вол
На стогнах шершавых от долгого сна шевелится.

121.

Когда городская выходит на стогны луна,
И медленно ей озаряется город дремучий,
И ночь нарастает, унынья и меди полна,
И грубому времени воск уступает певучий;

И плачет кукушка на каменной башне своей,
И бледная жница, сходящая в мир бездыханный,
Тихонько шевелит огромные спицы теней,
И желтой соломой бросает на пол деревянный ...

123.

Я в хоровод теней, топтавших нежный луг,
С певучим именем вмешался,
Но всё растаяло, и только слабый звук
В туманной памяти остался.

Сначала думал я, что имя — серафим,
И тела легкого дичился,
Немного дней прошло, и я смешался с ним
И в милой тени растворился.

И снова яблоня теряет дикий плод,
И тайный образ мне мелькает,
И богохульствует, и сам себя клянет,
И угли ревности глотает.

А счастье катится, как обруч золотой,
Чужую волю исполняя,
И ты гоняешься за легкою весной,
Ладонью воздух рассекая.

И так устроено, что не выходим мы
Из заколдованного круга.
Земли девической упругие холмы
Лежат спеленутые туго.

124.

Люблю под сводами седыя тишины
Молебнов, панихид блужданье,
И трогательный чин, ему же все должны
У Исаака отпеванье.

Люблю священника неторопливый шаг,
Широкий вынос плащаницы
И в ветхом неводе Генисаретский мрак
Великопостныя седмицы.

Ветхозаветный дым на теплых алтарях
И иерея возглас сирый,
Смиренник царственный: снег чистый на плечах
И одичалые порфиры.

Соборы вечные Софии и Петра,
Амбары воздуха и света,
Зернохранилища вселенского добра
И риги Нового Завета.

Не к вам влечется дух в годины тяжких бед,
Сюда влачится по ступеням
Широкопасмурным несчастья волчий след,
Ему вовеки не изменим:

Зане свободен раб, преодолевший страх,
И сохранилось свыше меры
В прохладных житницах, в глубоких закромах
Зерно глубокой, полной веры.

126.

Умывался ночью на дворе —
Твердь сияла грубыми звездами.
Звездный луч, как соль на топоре,
Стынет бочка с полными краями.

На замок закрыты ворота, .
И земля по совести сурова, —
Чище правды свежего холста
Вряд ли где отыщется основа.

Тает в бочке, словно соль, звезда,
И вода студеная чернее,
Чище смерть, соленее беда,
И земля правдивей и страшнее.

127.

Кому зима, арак и пунш голубоглазый,
Кому душистое с корицею вино,
Кому жестоких звезд соленые приказы
В избушку дымную перенести дано.

Немного теплого куриного помета
И бестолкового овечьего тепла;
Я всё отдам за жизнь — мне так нужна забота —
И спичка серная меня б согреть могла.

Взгляни: в моей руке лишь глиняная крынка,
И верещанье звезд щекочет слабый слух,
Но желтизну травы и теплоту суглинка
Нельзя не полюбить сквозь этот жалкий пух.

Тихонько гладить шерсть и ворошить солому,
Как яблоня зимой в рогоже голодать,
Тянуться с нежностью бессмысленно к чужому
И шарить в пустоте, и терпеливо ждать.

Пусть заговорщики торопятся по снегу
Отарою овец, и хрупкий наст скрипит,
Кому зима — полынь и горький дым — к ночлегу,
Кому — крутая соль торжественных обид.

О если бы поднять фонарь на длинной палке,
С собакой впереди идти под солью звезд,
И с петухом в горшке придти на двор к гадалке,
А белый, белый снег до боли очи ест.

128.

С розовой пеной усталости у мягких губ
Яростно волны зеленые роет бык,
Фыркает, гребли не любит — женолюб,
Ноша хребту непривычна, и труд велик.

Изредка выскочит дельфина колесо
Да повстречается морской колючий еж,
Нежные руки Европы — берите всё,
Где ты для выи желанней ярмо найдешь.

Горько внимает Европа могучий плеск,
Тучное море кругом закипает в ключ,
Видно, страшит ее вод маслянистых блеск,
И соскользнуть бы хотелось с шершавых
круч.

О, сколько раз ей милее уключин скрип,
Лоном широкая палуба, гурт овец,
И за высокой кормою мельканье рыб —
С нею безвесельный дальше плывет гребец!

130.

Как растет хлебов опара,
По началу хороша,
И беснуется от жару
Домовитая душа, —

Словно хлебные Софии
С херувимского стола
Круглым жаром налитые
Подымают купола.

Чтобы силой или лаской
Чудный выманить припек,
Время — царственный подпасок —
Ловит слово-колобок.

И свое находит место
Черствый пасынок веков —
Усыхающий довесок
Прежде вынутых хлебов.

131.

Я не знаю, с каких пор
Эта песенка началась —
Не по ней ли шуршит вор,
Комариный звенит князь?

Я хотел бы ни о чем
Еще раз поговорить,
Прошуршать спичкой, плечом
Растолкать ночь — разбудить.

Приподнять, как душный стог,
Воздух, что шапкой томит.
Перетряхнуть мешок,
В котором тмин зашит,

Чтобы розовой крови связь,
Этих сухоньких трав звон,
Уворованная нашлась
Через век, сеновал, сон.

132.

Я по лесенке приставной
Лез на всклокоченный сеновал, —
Я дышал звезд млечных трухой,
Колтуном пространства дышал.

И подумал: зачем будить
Удлиненных звучаний рой,
В этой вечной склоке ловить
Эолийский чудесный строй?

Звезд в ковше Медведицы семь.
Добрых чувств на земле пять.
Набухает, звенит темь,
И растет и звенит опять.

Распряженный огромный воз
Поперек вселенной торчит,
Сеновала древний хаос
Защекочет, запорошит.

Не своей чешуей шуршим,
Против шерсти мира поём.
Лиру строим, словно спешим
Обрасти косматым руном.

Из гнезда упавших щеглов
Косари приносят назад, —
Из горящих вырвусь рядов
И вернусь в родной звукоряд,

Чтобы розовой крови связь
И травы сухорукий звон
Распростились: одна скрепясь,
А другая — в заумный сон.

135. ВЕК

Век мой, зверь мой, кто сумеет
Заглянуть в твои зрачки
И своею кровью склеит
Двух столетий позвонки?
Кровь-строительница хлещет
Горлом из земных вещей,
Захребетник лишь трепещет
На пороге новых дней.

Тварь, покуда жизнь хватает,
Донести хребет должна,
И невидимым играет
Позвоночником волна.
Словно нежный хрящ ребенка —
Век младенческой земли,
Снова в жертву, как ягненка,
Темя жизни принесли.

Чтобы вырвать век из плена,
Чтобы новый мир начать,
Узловатых дней колена
Нужно флейтою связать.

Это век волну колышит
Человеческой тоской,
И в траве гадюка дышит
Мерой века золотой.

И еще набухнут почки,
Брызнет зелени побег,
Но разбит твой позвоночник,
Мой прекрасный жалкий век.
И с бессмысленной улыбкой
Вспять глядишь, жесток и слаб,
Словно зверь, когда-то гибкий,
На следы своих же лап.

---

136. НАШЕДШИЙ ПОДКОВУ

Глядим на лес и говорим:
Вот лес корабельный, мачтовый,
Розовые сосны
До самой верхушки свободные от мохнатой ноши,
Им бы поскрипывать в бурю,
Одинокими пиниями
В разъяренном безлесном воздухе;
Под соленою пятою ветра устоит отвес, пригнанный к пляшущей палубе.
И мореплаватель,
В необузданной жажде пространства,
Влача через влажные рытвины хрупкий прибор геометра,
Сличит с притяженьем земного лона
Шероховатую поверхность морей.

А вдыхая запах
Смолистых слез, проступивших сквозь обшивку корабля,
Любуясь на доски
Заклепанные, слаженные в переборки
Не вифлеемским мирным плотником, а другим —
Отцом путешествий, другом морехода, —
Говорим:
И они стояли на земле,
Неудобной, как хребет осла,
Забывая верхушками о корнях,
На знаменитом горном кряже,
И шумели под пресным ливнем,
Безуспешно предлагая небу выменять на щепотку соли
Свой благородный груз.

С чего начать?
Всё трещит и качается.
Воздух дрожит от сравнений.
Ни одно слово не лучше другого,
Земля гудит метафорой,
И легкие двуколки,
В броской упряжи густых от натуги птичьих стай,
Разрываются на части,
Соперничая с храпящими любимцами ристалищ.
Трижды блажен, кто введет в песнь имя;
Украшенная названьем песнь

Дольше живет среди других —
Она отмечена среди подруг повязкой на лбу,
Исцеляющей от беспамятства, слишком сильного одуряющего запаха —
Будь то близость мужчины,
Или запах шерсти сильного зверя,
Или просто дух чобра, растертого между ладоней.

Воздух бывает темным, как вода, и всё живое в нем плавает как рыба,
Плавниками расталкивая сферу,
Плотную, упругую, чуть нагретую, —
Хрусталь, в котором движутся колеса и шарахаются лошади,
Влажный чернозем Нееры, каждую ночь распаханный заново
Вилами, трезубцами, мотыгами, плугами.
Воздух замешан так же густо, как земля, —
Из него нельзя выйти, а в него трудно войти.

Шорох пробегает по деревьям зеленой лаптой;
Дети играют в бабки позвонками умерших животных.
Хрупкое летоисчисление нашей эры подходит к концу.
Спасибо за то, что было:
Я сам ошибся, я сбился, запутался в счете.
Эра звенела, как шар золотой,
Полая, литая, никем не поддерживаемая,
На всякое прикосновение отвечала «да» и «нет».
Так ребенок отвечает:
«Я дам тебе яблоко», или: «Я не дам тебе яблока».
И лицо его точный слепок с голоса, который произносит эти слова.

Звук еще звенит, хотя причина звука исчезла.
Конь лежит в пыли и храпит в мыле,
Но крутой поворот его шеи
Еще сохраняет воспоминание о беге с разбросанными ногами —
Когда их было не четыре,
А по числу камней дороги,
Обновляемых в четыре смены
По числу отталкиваний от земли пышущего жаром иноходца.

Так,
Нашедший подкову
Сдувает с нее пыль
И растирает ее шерстью, пока она не заблестит,
Тогда
Он вешает ее на пороге,
Чтобы она отдохнула,
И больше уж ей не придется высекать искры из кремня.
Человеческие губы,
                          которым больше нечего сказать,
Сохраняют форму последнего сказанного слова,
И в руке остается ощущение тяжести,
Хотя кувшин
            наполовину расплескался,
                              пока его несли домой.

То, что я сейчас говорю, говорю не я,
А вырыто из земли, подобно зернам окаменелой пшеницы.
Одни
      на монетах изображают льва,
Другие —
        голову;

Разнообразные медные, золотые и бронзовые лепешки
С одинаковой почестью лежат в земле.
Век, пробуя их перегрызть, оттиснул на них свои зубы.
Время срезает меня, как монету,
И мне уж не хватает меня самого.

140. 1 ЯНВАРЯ 1924

Кто время целовал в измученное темя —
С сыновьей нежностью потом
Он будет вспоминать, как спать ложилось время
В сугроб пшеничный за окном.
Кто веку поднимал болезненные веки —
Два сонных яблока больших —
Он слышит вечно шум, когда взревели реки
Времен обманных и глухих.

Два сонных яблока у века-властелина
И глиняный прекрасный рот,
Но к млеющей руке стареющего сына
Он, умирая, припадет.
Я знаю, с каждым днем слабеет жизни выдох,
Еще немного, — оборвут
Простую песенку о глиняных обидах
И губы оловом зальют.

О глиняная жизнь! О умиранье века!
Боюсь, лишь тот поймет тебя,
В ком беспомощная улыбка человека,
Который потерял себя.
Какая боль — искать потерянное слово,
Больные веки поднимать
И с известью в крови, для племени чужого
Ночные травы собирать.

Век. Известковый слой в крови больного сына
Твердеет. Спит Москва, как деревянный ларь,
И некуда бежать от века-властелина . . .
Снег пахнет яблоком, как встарь.
Мне хочется бежать от моего порога.
Куда? На улице темно,
И, словно сыплют соль мощеною дорогой,
Белеет совесть предо мной.

По переулочкам, скворешням и застрехам,
Недалеко собравшись как-нибудь,
Я, рядовой седок, укрывшись рыбьим мехом,
Всё силюсь полость застегнуть.
Мелькает улица, другая,
И яблоком хрустит саней морозных звук,
Не поддается петелька тугая,
Всё время валится из рук.

Каким железным, скобяным товаром
Ночь зимняя гремит по улицам Москвы.
То мерзлой рыбою стучит, то хлещет паром
Из чайных розовых — как серебром плотвы.
Москва — опять Москва. Я говорю ей: «здравствуй!
Не обессудь, теперь уж не беда,
По старине я уважаю братство
Мороза крепкого и щучьего суда».

Пылает на снегу аптечная малина
И где-то щелкнул ундервуд;
Спина извозчика и снег на пол-аршина:
Чего тебе еще? Не тронут, не убьют.
Зима-красавица и в звездах небо козье
Рассыпалось и молоком горит,
И конским волосом о мерзлые полозья
Вся полость трется и звенит.

А переулочки коптили керосинкой,
Глотали снег, малину, лед,
Всё шелушится им советской сонатинкой,
Двадцатый вспоминая год.
Ужели я предам позорному злословью —
Вновь пахнет яблоком мороз —
Присягу чудную четвертому сословью
И клятвы крупные до слез?

Кого еще убьешь? Кого еще прославишь?
Какую выдумаешь ложь?
То ундервуда хрящ: скорее вырви клавиш —
И щучью косточку найдешь;
И известковый слой в крови больного сына
Растает, и блаженный брызнет смех...
Но пишущих машин простая сонатина —
Лишь тень сонат могучих тех.

203—215. АРМЕНИЯ

III

Ты красок себе пожелала —
И выхватил лапой своей
Рисующий лев из пенала
С полдюжины карандашей.

Страна москательных пожаров
И мертвых гончарных равнин,
Ты рыжебородых сардаров
Терпела средь камней и глин.

Вдали якорей и трезубцев,
Где жухлый почил материк,
Ты видела всех жизнелюбцев,
Всех казнелюбивых владык.

И крови моей не волнуя,
Как детский рисунок просты,
Здесь жены проходят, даруя
От львиной своей красоты.

Как люб мне язык твой зловещий,
Твои молодые гроба,
Где буквы — кузнечные клещи,
И каждое слово — скоба...

IV

Ах, ничего я не вижу, и бедное ухо оглохло,
Всех-то цветов мне осталось лишь сурик да хриплая охра.

И почему-то мне начало утро армянское сниться,
Думал — возьму посмотрю, как живет в Эривани синица,

Как нагибается булочник, с хлебом играющий в жмурки,
Из очага вынимает лавашные влажные шкурки...

Ах, Эривань, Эривань! Иль птица тебя рисовала,
Или раскрашивал лев, как дитя, из цветного пенала?

Ах, Эривань, Эривань! Не город — орешек каленый,
Улиц твоих большеротых кривые люблю вавилоны.

Я бестолковую жизнь, как мулла свой коран, замусолил,
Время свое заморозил и крови горячей не пролил.

Ах, Эривань, Эривань, ничего мне больше не надо,
Я не хочу твоего замороженного винограда!

Орущих камней государство —
Армения, Армения!
Хриплые горы к оружью зовущая —
Армения, Армения!

К трубам серебряным Азии вечно летящая —
Армения, Армения!
Солнца персидские деньги щедро раздариваю-
                                        щая —
Армения, Армения!

Лазурь да глина, глина да лазурь,
Чего ж тебе еще? Скорей глаза сощурь,
Как близорукий шах над перстнем бирюзовым,
Над книгой звонких глин, над книжною землей,
Над гнойной книгою, над глиной дорогой,
Которой мучимся как музыкой и словом.

---

261. БАТЮШКОВ

Словно гуляка с волшебною тростью,
Батюшков нежный со мною живет —
По переулкам шагает в Замостье,
Нюхает розу и Зафну поет.

Ни на минуту не веря в разлуку,
Кажется, я поклонился ему:
В светлой перчатке холодную руку
Я с лихорадочной завистью жму.

Он усмехнулся. Я молвил — спасибо, —
И не нашел от смущения слов:
Ни у кого — этих звуков изгибы,
И никогда — этот говор валов ...

Наше мученье и наше богатство,
Косноязычный, с собой он принес —
Шум стихотворства и колокол братства
И гармонический проливень слез.

И отвечал мне оплакавший Тасса:.
— Я к величаньям еще не привык;
Только стихов виноградное мясо
Мне освежило случайно язык.

Что ж, поднимай удивленные брови,
Ты, горожанин и друг горожан, —
Вечные сны, как образчики крови,
Переливай из стакана в стакан ...

---

164. АВТОПОРТРЕТ

В поднятьи головы крылатый
Намек. Но мешковат сюртук.
В закрытьи глаз, в покое рук
Тайник движенья непочатый.

Так вот кому летать и петь
И слова пламенная ковкость,
Чтоб прирожденную неловкость
Врожденным ритмом одолеть.

222.

С миром державным я был лишь ребячески связан,
Устриц боялся и на гвардейцев смотрел исподлобья —
И ни крупицей души я ему не обязан,
Как я ни мучил себя по чужому подобью.

С важностью глупой, насупившись, в митре бобровой
Я не стоял под египетским портиком банка
И над лимонной Невою под хруст сторублевой
Мне никогда, никогда не плясала цыганка.

Чуя грядущие казни, от рева событий мятежных
Я убежал к нереидам на Черное море,
И от красавиц тогдашних, — от тех европеянок
                                        нежных —
Сколько я принял смущенья, надсады и горя!

Так отчего ж до сих пор этот город довлеет
Мыслям и чувствам моим по старинному праву?
Он от пожаров еще и морозов наглее,
Самолюбивый, проклятый, пустой, моложавый!

Не потому ль, что я видел на детской картинке
Лэди Годиву с распущенной рыжею гривой,
Я повторяю еще про себя под сурдинку:
Лэди Годива, прощай ... Я не помню, Годива ...

227.

За гремучую доблесть грядущих веков,
За высокое племя людей
Я лишился и чаши на пире отцов,
И веселья и чести своей.

Мне на плечи кидается век-волкодав,
Но не волк я по крови своей,
Запихай меня лучше, как шапку, в рукав
Жаркой шубы сибирских степей, —

Чтоб не видеть ни труса, ни хлипкой грязцы,
Ни кровавых костей в колесе,
Чтоб сияли всю ночь голубые песцы
Мне в своей первобытной красе.

Уведи меня в ночь, где течет Енисей,
И сосна до звезды достает,
Потому что не волк я по крови своей
И меня только равный убьет.

233.

Я пью за военные астры, за все, чем корили меня:
За барскую шубу, за астму, за желчь петербургского дня,

За музыку сосен савойских, Полей Елисейских бензин,
За розы в кабине ролс-ройса, за масло парижских картин.

Я пью за бискайские волны, за сливок альпийских кувшин,
За рыжую спесь англичанок и дальних колоний хинин,

Я пью, но еще не придумал, из двух выбираю одно:
Веселое асти-спуманте иль папского замка вино...

223.

Помоги, Господь, эту ночь прожить:
Я за жизнь боюсь — за Твою рабу —
В Петербурге жить — словно спать в гробу.

258. ИМПРЕССИОНИЗМ

Художник нам изобразил
Глубокий обморок сирени,
И красок звучные ступени
На холст, как струпья, положил.

Он понял масла густоту —
Его запекшееся лето
Лиловым мозгом разогрето,
Расширенное в духоту.

А тень-то, тень все лиловей —
Смычек иль хлыст, как спичка,
                                            тухнет, —
Ты скажешь: повара на кухне
Готовят жирных голубей.

Угадывается качель,
Недомалеваны вуали,
И в этом солнечном развале
Уже хозяйничает шмель.

267. АРИОСТ

Во всей Италии приятнейший, умнейший,
Любезный Ариост немножечко охрип.
Он наслаждается перечисленьем рыб
И перчит все моря нелепицею злейшей.

И, словно музыкант на десяти цимбалах,
Не уставая рвать повествований нить,
Ведет туда-сюда, не зная сам, как быть,
Запутанный рассказ о рыцарских скандалах.

На языке цикад пленительная смесь
Из грусти пушкинской и средиземной спеси.
Он завирается, с Орландом куролеся,
И содрогается, преображаясь весь.

И морю говорит: — Шуми без всяких дум.
И деве на скале: — Лежи без покрывала...
Рассказывай еще — тебя нам слишком мало,
Покуда в жилах кровь, в ушах покуда шум...

О город ящериц, в котором нет души!
Когда бы чаще ты таких мужей рожала,
Феррара черствая... Который раз сначала,
Покуда в жилах кровь, рассказывай, спеши...

В Европе холодно, в Италии темно.
Власть отвратительна, как руки брадобрея.
А он вельможится все лучше, все хитрее
И улыбается в открытое окно

Ягненку на горе, монаху на осляти,
Солдатам герцога, юродивым слегка
От винопития, чумы и чеснока,
И в сетке синих мух уснувшему дитяти.

А я люблю его неистовый досуг —
Язык бессмысленный, язык солено-сладкий
И звуков стакнутых прелестные двойчатки,
Боюсь раскрыть ножом двухстворчатый жемчуг.

Любезный Ариост, быть может, век пройдет —
В одно широкое и братское лазорье
Сольем твою лазурь и наше черноморье.
И мы бывали там. И мы там пили мед.

268. АРИОСТ [Вариант]

В Европе холодно. В Италии темно.
Власть отвратительна, как руки брадобрея.
О, если б распахнуть, да как нельзя скорее,
На Адриатику широкое окно.

Над розой мускусной жужжание пчелы,
В степи полуденной — кузнечик мускулистый,
Крылатой лошади подковы тяжелы,
Часы песочные желты и золотисты.

На языке цикад пленительная смесь
Из грусти пушкинской и средиземной спеси,
Как плющ назойливый, цепляющийся весь,
Он мужественно врет, с Орландом куролеся.

Часы песочные желты и золотисты,
В степи полуденной кузнечик мускулистый,
И прямо на луну взлетает враль плечистый ...

Любезный Ариост, посольская лиса,
Цветущий папоротник, парусник, столетник,
Ты слушал на луне овсянок голоса,
А на дворе у рыб ученый был советник.

О город ящериц, в котором нет души!
От ведьмы и судьи таких сынов рожала
Феррара черствая и на цепи держала —
И солнце рыжего ума взошло в глуши!

Мы удивляемся лавчонке мясника,
Под сеткой синих мух уснувшему дитяти,
Ягненку на горе, монаху на осляти,
Солдатам герцога, юродивым слегка
От винопития, чумы и чеснока,
И свежи, как заря, удивлены утрате.

286.

Мы живем, под собою не чуя страны,
Наши речи за десять шагов не слышны,

А где хватит на полразговорца, —
Там припомнят кремлевского горца.

Его толстые пальцы, как черви, жирны,
А слова, как пудовые гири, верны.

Тараканьи смеются усища,
И сияют его голенища.

А вокруг его сброд тонкошеих вождей,
Он играет услугами полулюдей.

Кто свистит, кто мяучит, кто хнычет,
Он один лишь бабачит и тычет.

Как подковы кует за указом указ —
Кому в пах, кому в лоб, кому в бровь, кому
                                                      в глаз.

Что ни казнь у него, — то малина
И широкая грудь осетина.

130

ПУТЕШЕСТВИЕ В АРМЕНИЮ

АЛАГЕЗ

1. Тело Аршака не умыто и борода его одичала.

2. Ногти царя сломаны, и по лицу его ползают мокрицы.

3. Уши его поглупели от тишины, а когда-то они слушали греческую музыку.

4. Язык опаршивел от пищи тюремщиков, а было время — он прижимал виноградины к нёбу и был ловок, как кончик языка флейтиста.

5. Семя Аршака зачахло в мошонке и голос его жидок, как блеяние овцы . . .

6. Царь Шапух, — так думает Аршак, — взял верх надо мной и — хуже того — он взял мой воздух себе.

7. Ассириец держит мое сердце.

8. Он — начальник волос моих и ногтей моих. Он отпускает мне бороду и глотает слюну мою, — до того привык он к мысли, что я нахожусь здесь — в крепости Аньюш.

9. Народ Кушани возмутился против Шапуха.

10. Они прорвали границу в незащищенном месте, как шелковый шнур.

11. Наступление Кушани кололо и беспокоило царя Шапуха, как ресница, попавшая в глаз.

12. Обе стороны (враги) зажмурились, чтобы не видеть друг друга.

13. Некий Дармастат, самый образованный и любезный из евнухов, был в середине войска Шапуха, ободрял командующего конницей, подольстился к владыке, вывел его, как шахматную фигуру, из опасности и все время держался на виду.

14. Он был губернатором провинции Андех в те дни, когда Аршак бархатным голосом отдавал приказания.

15. Вчера был царь, а сегодня провалился в щель, скрючился в утробе, как младенец, согревается вшами и наслаждается чесоткой.

16. Когда дошло до награждения, Дармастат вложил в острые уши ассирийца просьбу, щекочущую, как перо:

17. Дай мне пропуск в крепость Аньюш. Я хочу, чтобы Аршак провел один добавочный день, полный слышанья, вкуса и обонянья, как бывало раньше, когда он развлекался охотой и заботился о древонасаждении.

296.

Твоим узким плечам под бичами краснеть,
Под бичами краснеть, на морозе гореть.

Твоим детским рукам утюги поднимать,
Утюги поднимать да веревки вязать.

Твоим нежным ногам по стеклу босиком,
По стеклу босиком да кровавым песком.

Ну а мне за тебя черной свечкой гореть,
Черной свечкой гореть да молиться не сметь.

299. ЧЕРНОЗЕМ

Переуважена, перечерна, вся в холе,
Вся в холках маленьких, вся воздух и призор,
Вся рассыпаючись, вся образуя хор —
Комочки влажные моей земли и воли!

В дни ранней пахоты — черна до синевы,
И безоружная в ней зиждится работа —
Тысячехолмия распаханной молвы —
Знать, безокружное в окружности есть что-то!

И все-таки земля — проруха и обух —
Не умолить ее, как в ноги ей ни бухай:
Гниющей флейтою настраживает слух,
Кларнетом утренним зазябливает ухо.

Как на лемех приятен жирный пласт,
Как степь молчит в апрельском провороте . . .
Ну, здравствуй, чернозем, будь мужествен,
                                                   глазаст —
Черноречивое молчание в работе.

306.

Да, я лежу в земле, губами шевеля,
Но то, что я скажу, заучит каждый школьник:

На Красной площади всего круглей земля
И скат ее твердеет добровольный,

На Красной площади земля всего круглей,
И скат ее нечаянно раздольный,

Откидываясь вниз до рисовых полей,
Покуда на земле последний жив невольник.

307.

Лишив меня морей, разбега и разлета
И дав стопе упор насильственной земли,
Чего добились вы? Блестящего расчета:
Губ шевелящихся отнять вы не могли.

312. СТАНСЫ

(6)

Моя страна со мною говорила,
Мирволила, журила, не прочла,
Но возмужавшего меня, как очевидца,
Заметила — и вдруг, как чечевица,
Адмиралтейским лучиком зажгла.

316.

Римских ночей полновесные слитки,
Юношу Гете манившее лоно,

Пусть я в ответе, но не в убытке —
Есть многодонная жизнь вне закона.

319.

Бежит волна — волной волне хребет ломая,
Кидаясь на луну в невольничьей тоске,
И янычарская пучина молодая —
Неусыпленная столица волновая —
Кривеет, мечется и роет ров в песке.

А через воздух сумрачно-хлопчатый
Неначатой стены мерещятся зубцы,
И с пенных лестниц падают солдаты
Султанов мнительных — разбрызганы, разъ-
                                                   яты, —
И яд разносят хладные скопцы.

318.

Исполню дымчатый обряд:
В опале предо мной лежат
Морского лета земляники —
Двуискренние сердолики
И муравьиный брат — агат,
Но мне милей простой солдат
Морской пучины — серый, дикий,
Которому никто не рад.

320.

Не мучнистой бабочкою белой
В землю я заемный прах верну.
Я хочу, чтоб мыслящее тело
Превратилось в улицу, в страну —
Позвоночное, обугленное тело,
Осознавшее свою длину.

Возгласы темнозеленой хвои —
С глубиной колодезной венки —
Тянут жизнь и время дорогое,
Опершись на смертные станки,
Обручи краснознаменной хвои —
Азбучные, круглые венки.

Шли товарищи последнего призыва
По работе в жестких небесах,
Пронесла пехота молчаливо
Восклицанья ружей на плечах.

И зенитных тысячи орудий —
Карих то зрачков иль голубых —
Шли нестройно — люди, люди, люди —
Кто же будет продолжать за них?

329.

Нынче день какой-то желторотый:
Не могу его понять —
И глядят приморские ворота
В якорях, в туманах на меня.

Тихий, тихий по воде линялой
Ход военных кораблей,
И каналов узкие пеналы
Подо льдом еще черней.

336.

Как подарок запоздалый,
Ощутима мной зима:
Я люблю ее сначала
Неуверенный размах.

Хороша она испугом,
Как начало грозных дел:
Перед всем безлесным кругом
Даже ворон оробел.

Но сильней всего непрочно —
Выпуклых голубизна:
Полукруглый лед височный
Речек, бающих без сна . . .

СТИХИ О СТАЛИНЕ

1

Когда б я уголь взял для высшей похвалы –
Для радости рисунка непреложной, –
Я б воздух расчертил на хитрые углы
И осторожно и тревожно,
Чтоб настоящее в чертах отозвалось,
В искусстве с дерзостью больша
Я б рассказал о том, кто сдвинул мира ось,
Ста сорока народов чтя обычай.
Я б поднял брови малый уголек,
И поднял вновь и разрешил иначе:
Знать, Прометей раздул свой уголек, –
Гляди, Эсхил, как я рисуя плачу!

2

Я б несколько гремучих линий взял,
Все моложавое его тысячелетье,
И мужество улыбкою связал
И развязал в ненапряженном свете,
И в дружбе мудрых глаз найду для близнеца,
Какого не скажу, то выраженье, близясь
К которому, к нему – вдруг узнаешь отца
И задыхаешься, почуяв мира близость.
И я хочу благодарить холмы,
Что эту кость и эту кисть развили:
Он родился в горах и горечь знал тюрьмы.
Хочу назвать его – не Сталин, – Джугашвили!

3

Художник, береги и охраняй бойца:
В рост окружи его сырым и синим бором
Вниманья влажного. Не огорчить отца
Недобрым образом иль мыслей недобором.
Художник, помоги тому, кто весь с тобой,
Кто мыслит, чувствует и строит.
Не я и не другой – ему народ родной,
Народ-Гомер хвалу утроит.
Художник, береги и охраняй бойца:
Лес человечества за ним идет густея,
Само грядущее – дружина мудреца –
И слушает его все чаще, все смелее.

4

Он свесился с трибуны как с горы
В бугры голов: должник сильнее иска.
Могучие глаза решительно добры,
Густая бровь кому-то светит близко,
И я хотел бы стрелкой указать
На твердость рта – отца речей упрямых.
Лепное, сложное, крутое веко, знать,
Работает из миллиона рамок.
Весь откровенность, весь признанья медь,
И зоркий слух, не терпящий сурдинки,
На всех готовых жить и умереть
Бегут играя хмурые морщинки.

5

Сжимая уголек, в котором все сошлось,
Рукою жадною одно лишь сходство клича,
Рукою хищною – ловить лишь сходства ось,
Я уголь искрошу, ища его обличья,
Я у него учусь к себе не знать пощады,
Несчастья скроют ли большого плана часть,
Я разыщу его в случайностях их чада.,, .

. . .

Пусть недостоин я еще иметь друзей,
Пусть не насыщен я и желчью и слезами,
Он все мне чудится в шинели, в картузе,
На чудной площади с счастливыми глазами.

6

Глазами Сталина раздвинута гора
И вдаль прищурилась равнина.
Как море без морщин, как завтра из вчера –
До солнца борозды от плуга-исполина.
Он улыбается улыбкой жнеца
Рукопожатий в разговоре,
Который начался и длится без конца
На шестиклятвенном просторе.
И каждое гумно и каждая копна
Сильна, убориста, умна – добро живое –
Чудо народное! Да будет жизнь крупна.
Ворочается счастье стержневое.

7

И шестикратно я в сознаньи берегу,
Свидетель медленный труда, борьбы и жатвы,
Его огромный путь – через тайгу
И Ленинский Октябрь – до выполненной клятвы.
Уходят вдаль людских голов бугры:
Я уменьшаюсь там, меня уж не заметят,
Но в книгах ласковых и в играх детворы
Воскресну я сказать, что солнце светит.
Правдивей правды нет, чем искренность бойца:
Для чести и любви, для воздуха и стали
Есть имя славное для сильных губ чтеца –
Его мы слышали и им его застали.

354.

Еще не умер я, еще я не один,
Покуда с нищенкой-подругой
Я наслаждаюсь величием равнин
И мглой, и голодом, и вьюгой.

В прекрасной бедности, в роскошной нищете
Живу один — спокоен и утешен —
Благословенны дни и ночи те,
И сладкозвучный труд безгрешен.

Несчастен тот, кого, как тень его,
Пугает лай и ветер косит,
И беден тот, кто, сам полуживой,
У тени милостыни просит.

349.

В лицо морозу я гляжу один:
Он — никуда, я — ниоткуда,
И все утюжится, плоится без морщин
Равнины дышащее чудо.

А солнце щурится в крахмальной нищете —
Его прищур спокоен и утешен...
Десятизначные леса почти что те...
А снег хрустит в глазах, как чистый хлеб
                                        безгрешен.

351.

О, этот медленный, одышливый простор —
Я им пресыщен до отказа! —
И отдышавшийся распахнут кругозор —
Повязку бы на оба глаза!

Уж лучше б вынес я песка слоистый нрав
На берегах зубчатых Камы,
Я б удержал ее застенчивый рукав,
Ее круги, края и ямы.

Я б с ней сработался — на век, на миг один —
Стремнин осадистых завистник —
Я б слушал под корой текущих древесин
Ход кольцеванья волокнистый.

350.

Что делать нам с убитостью равнин,
С протяжным голодом их чуда?
Ведь то, что мы открытостью в них мним,
Мы сами видим, засыпая, зрим, —
И все растет вопрос — куда они? откуда? —
И не ползет ли медленно по ним
Тот, о котором мы во сне кричим, —
Народов будущих Иуда?

352.

Не сравнивай: живущий несравним.
С каким-то ласковым испугом
Я соглашался с равенством равнин,
И неба круг мне был недугом.

Я обращался к воздуху-слуге,
Ждал от него услуги или вести
И собирался в путь, и плавал по дуге
Неначинающихся путешествий.

Где больше неба мне — там я бродить готов —
И ясная тоска меня не отпускает
От молодых еще воронежских холмов
К всечеловеческим — яснеющим в Тоскане.

353.

Как женственное серебро горит,
Что с окисью и примесью боролось,
И тихая работа серебрит
Железный плуг и стихотворца голос.

341.

Уходят вдаль людских голов бугры,
Я уменьшаюсь там — меня уж не заметят,
Но в книгах ласковых и в играх детворы
Воскресну я сказать, что солнце светит.

358.

Слышу, слышу ранний лед,
Шелестящий под мостами,
Вспоминаю, как плывет
Светлый хмель над головами.

С черствых лестниц, с площадей
С угловатыми дворцами
Круг Флоренции своей
Алигьери пел мощней
Утомленными губами.

Так гранит зернистый тот
Тень моя грызет очами,
Видит ночью ряд колод,
Днем казавшихся домами.

Или тень баклуши бьет
И позевывает с нами,

Иль шумит среди людей,
Греясь их вином и небом,

И несладким кормит хлебом
Неотвязных лебедей . . .

359.

Люблю морозное дыханье
И пара зимнего признанье:
Я — это я, явь — это явь!

И мальчик, красный как фонарик,
Своих салазок государик
И заправила, мчится вплавь.

И я — в размолвке с миром, с волей —
Заразе саночек мирволю
В сребристых скобках, в бахромах, —

И век бы падал векши легче,
И легче векши к мягкой речке, —
Полнеба в валенках, в ногах!

360.

Куда мне деться в этом январе?
Открытый город сумасбродно цепок . . .
От замкнутых я что ли пьян дверей? —
И хочется мычать от всех замков и
                                     скрепок.

И переулков лающих чулки,
И улиц перекошенных чуланы,
И прячутся поспешно в уголки,
И выбегают из углов угланы.

И в яму, в бородавчатую темь
Скольжу к обледенелой водокачке,
И, спотыкаясь, мертвый воздух ем,
И разлетаются грачи в горячке.

А я за ними ахаю, стуча
В какой-то мерзлый деревянный короб:
— Читателя! советчика! врача!
На лестнице колючей — разговора б!

265.

Сегодня можно снять декалькомани,
Мизинец окунув в Москву-реку,
С разбойника-Кремля. Какая прелесть
Фисташковые эти голубятни —
Хоть проса им насыпать, хоть овса!
А в недорослях кто? Иван Великий —
Великовозрастная колокольня,
Стоит себе еще болван-болваном
Который век. Его бы заграницу,
Чтоб доучился. Да куда там!.. Стыдно.

Река-Москва в четырехтрубном дыме,
И перед нами весь раскрытый город —
Купальщики-заводы и сады
Замоскворецкие. Не так ли,
Откинув палисандровую крышку
Огромного концертного рояля,
Мы проникаем в звучное нутро?
Белогвардейцы, вы его видали?
Рояль Москвы слыхали? Гули-гули!

Мне кажется, как всякое другое,
Ты — время, незаконно . . . Как мальчишка,
За взрослыми в морщинистую воду,
Я, кажется, в грядущее вхожу,
И, кажется, его я не увижу.

Уж я не выйду в ногу с молодежью
На разлинованные стадионы.
Разбуженный повесткой мотоцикла,
Я на рассвете не вскочу с постели,
В стеклянные дворцы на курьих ножках
Я даже тенью легкой не войду.

Мне с каждым днем дышать все тяжелее,
А между тем нельзя повременить —
Ведь рождены для наслажденья бегом
Лишь сердце человека и коня . . .

А Фауста бес — сухой и моложавый —
Вновь старику кидается в ребро,
И подбивает взять почасно ялик,
Или махнуть на Воробьевы горы,
Иль на трамвае охлестнуть Москву . . .
Ей некогда: она сегодня в няньках —
Все мечется на сорок тысяч люлек,
Она одна и пряжа на руках.

364.

Как светотени мученик Рембрандт,
Я глубоко ушел в немеющее время,
Но резкость моего горящего ребра
Не охраняется ни сторожами теми,
Ни этим воином, что под грозою спят.

Простишь ли ты меня, великолепный брат,
И мастер, и отец чернозеленой теми,
Но око соколиного пера
И жаркие ларцы у полночи в гареме
Смущают не к добру, смущают без добра
Мехами сумрака взволнованное племя.

366.

Разрывы круглых бухт и хрящ и синева,
И парус медленный, что облаком продолжен —
Я с вами разлучен, вас оценив едва:
Длиннｅй органных фуг — горька морей трава
Ложноволосая — и пахнет долгой ложью.
Железной нежностью хмелеет голова,
И ржавчина чуть-чуть отлогий берег гложет ...
Что ж мне под голову другой песок подложен?
Ты — горловой Урал, плечистое Поволжье
Иль этот ровный край — вот все мои права, —
И полной грудью их вдыхать еще я должен.

365.

Пою, когда гортань сыра, душа суха,
И в меру влажен взор, и не хитрит сознанье.
Здорово ли вино? Здоровы ли меха?
Здорово ли в крови Колхиды колыханье?
А грудь стесняется, без языка тиха:
Уже не я пою, — поет мое дыханье —
И в горных ножнах слух и голова глуха.

Песнь бескорыстная сама себе хвала,
Утеха для друзей и для врагов смола.

Песнь одноглазая, растущая из мха,
Одноголосый дар охотничьего быта,
Которую поют верхом и на верхах,
Держа дыханье вольно и открыто,
Заботясь лишь о том, чтоб честно и сердито
На свадьбу молодых доставить без греха ...

368.

Были очи острее точимой косы —
По зегзице в зенице и по капле росы, —

И едва научились они во весь рост
Различать одинокое множество звезд.

367.

Вооруженный зреньем узких ос,
Сосущих ось земную, ось земную,
Я чую все, с чем свидеться пришлось,
И вспоминаю наизусть и всуе.

И не рисую я, и не пою,
И не вожу смычком черноголосым:
Я только в жизнь впиваюсь и люблю
Завидовать могучим хитрым осам.

О, если б и меня когда-нибудь могло
Заставить, сон и смерть минуя,
Стрекало воздуха и летнее тепло
Услышать ось земную, ось земную ...

370.

Я в львиный ров и в крепость погружен
И опускаюсь ниже, ниже, ниже
Под этих звуков ливень дрожжевой —
Сильнее льва, мощнее Пятикнижья.

Как близко-близко твой подходит зов —
До заповедей роды и первины —
Океанийских низка жемчугов
И таитянок кроткие корзины.

Карающего пенья материк,
Густого голоса низинами надвинься!
Всех наших дочерей дикарско-сладкий лик
Не стоит твоего — праматери — мизинца.

Неограничена еще моя пора,
И я сопровождал восторг вселенский
Как вполголосная органная игра
Сопровождает голос женский.

372.

Если б меня наши враги взяли
И перестали со мной говорить люди;
Если б лишили меня всего в мире —
Права дышать и открывать двери
И утверждать, что бытие будет,
И что народ, как судия, судит;
Если б меня смели держать зверем,
Пищу мою на пол кидать бы стали б, —
Я не смолчу, не заглушу боли,
Но начерчу то, что чертить волен,
И раскачав колокол стен голый,
И разбудив вражеской тьмы угол,
Я запрягу десять волов в голос
И поведу руку во тьме плугом,
И, в океан братских очей сжатый,
Я упаду тяжестью всей жатвы,
Сжатостью всей рвущейся вдаль клятвы,

И в глубине сторожевой ночи
Чернорабочей вспыхнут земли очи,
И промелькнет пламенных лет стая,
Прошелесят спелой грозой — Ленин,
И по земле, что избежит тленья,
Будет будить разум и жизнь — Сталин.

380.

Может быть, это точка безумия,
Может быть, это совесть твоя:
Узел жизни, в котором мы узнаны
И развязаны для бытия.

Так соборы кристаллов сверхжизненных
Добросовестный луч-паучок,
Распуская на ребра, их сызнова
Собирает в единый пучок.

Чистых линий пучки благодарные,
Собираемы тонким лучом,
Соберутся, сойдутся когда-нибудь,
Словно гости с открытым челом.

Только здесь на земле, а не на́ небе,
Как в наполненный музыкой дом. —
Только их не спугнуть, не изранить бы —
Хорошо, если мы доживем.

То, что я говорю, мне прости,
Тихо, тихо его мне прочти.

384.

О, как же я хочу —
Нечуемый никем —
Лететь вослед лучу,
Где нет меня совсем.

А ты в кругу лучись —
Другого счастья нет —
И у звезды учись
Тому, что значит свет.

А я тебе хочу
Сказать, что я шепчу,
Что шёпотом лучу
Тебя, дитя, вручу.

Он только тем и луч,
Он только тем и свет,
Что шёпотом могуч
И лепетом согрет.

385.

Гончарами велик остров синий —
Крит веселый, запекся их дар
В землю звонкую. Слышишь дельфиний
Плавников их подземный удар?

Это море легко на помине
В осчастливленной обжигом глине,
И сосуда студеная власть
Раскололась на море и глаз.

Ты отдай мне мое, остров синий,
Крит летучий, отдай мне мой труд,
И сосцами текучей богини
Напои обожженный сосуд.

Это было и пелось, синея,
Много задолго до Одиссея,
До того, как еду и питье
Называли «моя» и «мое».

Выздоравливай же, излучайся,
Волоокого неба звезда,
И летучая рыба — случайность,
И вода, говорящая «да».

387.

Флейты греческой тэта и йота —
Словно ей нехватало молвы —
Неизваянная, без отчета,
Зрела, маялась, шла через рвы.

И ее невозможно покинуть,
Стиснув зубы ее не унять,
И в слова языком не продвинуть,
И губами ее не размять.

А флейтист не узнает покоя —
Ему кажется, что он один,
Что когда-то он море родное
Из сиреневых вылепил глин.

Звонким шепотом честолюбивым,
Вспоминающим топотом губ
Он торопится быть бережливым,
Емлет звуки, опрятен и скуп.

Вслед за ним мы его не повторим,
Комья глины в ладонях моря,
И когда я наполнился морем,
Мором стала мне мера моя.

И свои-то мне губы не любы,
И убийство на том же корню.
И невольно на убыль, на убыль
Равнодействия флейты клоню.

388.

Я к губам подношу эту зелень,
Эту клейкую клятву листов,
Эту клятвопреступную землю —
Мать подснежников, кленов, дубков.

Погляди, как я слепну и крепну,
Подчиняясь смиренным корням,
И не слишком ли великолепно
От гремучего парка глазам?

А квакуши, как шарики ртути,
Голосами сцепляются в шар,
И становятся ветками прутья
И молочною выдумкой — пар.

394.

К пустой земле невольно припадая
Неравномерной сладостной походкой,
Она идет, чуть-чуть опережая
Подругу быструю и юношу-погодка.
Ее влечет стесненная свобода
Одушевляющего недостатка,
И кажется, что ясная догадка
В ее походке хочет задержаться —
О том, что эта вешняя погода
Для нас праматерь гробового свода,
И это будет вечно начинаться.

Есть женщины сырой земле родные,
И каждый шаг их — гулкое рыданье,
Сопровождать умерших и впервые
Приветствовать воскресших — их призванье.
И ласки требовать у них преступно,
И расставаться с ними непосильно.
Сегодня — ангел, завтра — червь могильный,
А послезавтра — только очертанье.
Что было — поступь, — станет недоступно,
Цветы бессмертны. Небо целокупно.
И то, что будет — только обещанье.

Index of first lines
and titles

Numbers in brackets are those of *Sobraniye sochineniy (Collected Works)*, edited by G.P.Struve and B.A.Filippov, second edition, Washington, 1967.